[C]hildren must ever be cherished,
for they are not only the hope
and the promise of my people:
with them stands the destiny
of democracy in America.

— Paul Robeson

THE COVENANT *In Action*

THE COVENANT *In Action*

Compiled by Tavis Smiley

SMILEY BOOKS

SMILEY BOOKS,
an imprint of Hay House, Inc.

Carlsbad, California
Sydney • London • Johannesburg
Vancouver • Hong Kong • New Delhi

Send inquiries to: The Smiley Group, Inc., 3870 Crenshaw Blvd., Suite 391,
Los Angeles, CA 90008.

Library of Congress Control Number: 2006910864

ISBN 13: 978-1-4019-1852-1

10 09 08 07   4 3 2 1
1st edition, January 2007

Printed in the United States of America

CONTENTS

The Covenants ix

Acknowledgments xi

Foreword by Tavis Smiley xiii

Introduction:
A Conversation with Angela Glover Blackwell
and Stephanie Robinson xv

THE COVENANT *In Action:*
What Individuals and Communities Are Doing 1

THE COVENANT *In Action:*
Voices of Black America's Young Activists 19

THE COVENANT *In Action:*
The Toolkit for Next Steps 33

A Call to Action 89

Afterword by Cornel West 91

Appendix I: *The Covenant* Curriculum 93

Appendix II: African-American History Timeline 101

Appendix III: That's My Baby! 175

About Tavis Smiley 189

About Cornel West 190

THE COVENANTS

Covenant I:
Securing the Right to Healthcare and Well-Being

Covenant II:
Establishing a System of Public Education in Which All Children
Achieve at High Levels and Reach Their Full Potential

Covenant III:
Correcting the System of Unequal Justice

Covenant IV:
Fostering Accountable Community-Centered Policing

Covenant V:
Ensuring Broad Access to Affordable Neighborhoods
That Connect to Opportunity

Covenant VI:
Claiming Our Democracy

Covenant VII:
Strengthening Our Rural Roots

Covenant VIII:
Accessing Good Jobs, Wealth, and Economic Prosperity

Covenant IX:
Assuring Environmental Justice for All

Covenant X:
Closing the Racial Digital Divide

ACKNOWLEDGMENTS

THE COVENANT *In Action* was made possible through a strategic partnership with PolicyLink and The Jamestown Project.

We thank Natalie Gluck of PolicyLink for identifying, connecting with, and profiling some of the many people who are working to advance the goals of the *Covenant with Black America* and telling their stories so vividly in this book.

We thank Charisse Carney-Nunes for coordinating and writing on behalf of The Jamestown Project.

We are also especially grateful to both Natalie and Charisse for their dedication in identifying the young activists whose inspirational words of wisdom are shared on the pages that follow.

In addition, we thank Paulette Jones Robinson, a longtime consultant to PolicyLink for her superb editing of this document; Professor Paul C. Taylor, Senior Fellow for The Jamestown Project; Enola Aird, The Jamestown Project Advisory Board Member; Brandi Colander, Research Associate for The Jamestown Project; and Milly Hawk Daniel, Vice President of Communications for PolicyLink, for their important contributions.

Finally, this text and related *Covenant* projects would not be possible without the invaluable input of Ken Browning, Martin Erb, Sheryl Flowers, Amy Rose Grigoriou, Jill Kramer, Kimberly McFarland, Denise Pines, Christy Salinas, Stev Stephens, and Reid Tracy.

FOREWORD
by Tavis Smiley

Perhaps you've heard me say that "life is not about the breaths we take, but rather the moments that take our breath away." The response of the black community to the *Covenant with Black America* has indeed been breathtaking. My heart is filled with encouragement when I reflect on the past year.

The book just caught fire throughout the nation. Immediately following the release of *The Covenant* in Houston in February 2006, I began what I thought would be a six- or seven-city tour to talk with black people about the book and the issues we are facing as a people. I was amazed by the many thousands of people who came out to churches and community venues to talk about *The Covenant* goals and the future of Black America. In response to demand, we expanded the tour to about 20 cities, and I wish I could have done more. The hunger to talk about these issues was vast; and the conversations were rich, revealing, and urgent. It seemed that everybody everywhere wanted to read and talk about the *Covenant with Black America!*

Within a month of its release, *The Covenant* hit number 1 on the bestsellers lists of Barnes and Noble, Borders, *The Washington Post*, *The Los Angeles Times*, *USA Today*, and even the *New York Times Book Review*, where it not only reached the top spot on the bestsellers list for Paperback/Nonfiction, but it also stayed on that list for 14 weeks. In September it reappeared on the *New York Times* bestsellers list, probably because so many students were purchasing the book as the school year began.

In fact, the book has made history as the first book published by a black publishing company to appear on any of the *New York Times* bestsellers lists. All of this proved what I had already known for sure—that black folk are thirsty for information about the state of Black America and for an action agenda they can use to address the issues that impact our communities.

I have been inspired by the actions black people have taken in response to *The Covenant*. Churches, civic associations, community organizations, elected officials, neighborhood leaders, and everyday people have picked up the challenge, offering helping hands to others and becoming activists, crusaders, and advocates for change. THE COVENANT *In Action* tells just a few of the stories of the wonderful things that Black Americans have done to advance *The Covenant* goals. It describes activities that have been instigated by *The Covenant*, and it offers profiles of young black activists who exemplify the quality of leadership that is emerging from the next generation.

Achieving *The Covenant* goals will also require the engagement of advocates who are willing to challenge the systems and institutions that make it difficult for black people to advance. We all have the capacity to be effective advocates. To encourage and increase that capacity, THE COVENANT *In Action* includes a toolkit to help us systematically take on the issues described in *The Covenant*, whether that means organizing a campaign to change a law, launching a media campaign to draw attention to racial inequity, or getting lawyers to file a lawsuit to address an injustice. Importantly, the toolkit includes innovative and creative techniques to assist communities in getting started, connecting with one another, and moving *Covenant* issues into action.

The *Covenant with Black America* will not truly be a success unless we realize its promise. To do that we must act, act as individuals to do what we can to improve our lives and the lives of those in our families and communities; that means becoming role models for the changes we seek, volunteering, mentoring, organizing for change, speaking out, holding leaders accountable, and becoming advocates for justice. I hope THE COVENANT *In Action* inspires and helps you to become part of *The Covenant* movement.

INTRODUCTION:

A Conversation with Angela Glover Blackwell
and Stephanie Robinson

THE COVENANT *In Action* was developed through a strategic partnership with PolicyLink and The Jamestown Project. Working together, these two organizations have produced this book to continue the inspirational spirit of the *Covenant with Black America* and to empower people to take effective action to achieve *The Covenant* goals. Both Jamestown and PolicyLink believe that the information, tools, and ideas presented in THE COVENANT *In Action* will enable and inspire people to become actual agents of change in their respective communities and to become partners in a larger *Covenant* movement.

THE COVENANT *In Action* is organized into three parts: (1) stories about the projects and actions that everyday people have undertaken over the past year that were inspired by the *Covenant with Black America;* (2) motivational essays from young black activists on the ground impacting their environments; and (3) a toolkit outlining steps you can take to organize, agitate, connect, and act. The toolkit contains not only traditional action strategies, but also includes innovative approaches to organizing and community building that will result in stronger, more bonded communities that are reflective of their history and past experiences and ready to make change. The *Covenant with Black America* was only the first step. The toolkit will prime and prepare you to actually move *The Covenant* into action.

Angela Glover Blackwell, a major contributor to the *Covenant with Black America*, is the Founder and CEO of PolicyLink, a national, non-profit research and action institute working collaboratively to achieve economic and social equity. She has 30 years of experience as an organizer, a public-interest lawyer, a community builder, a foundation executive, and a policy advocate. Working from the wisdom, voice, and experience of those leading change in their communities, Policy-Link is demonstrating new ways to create a society in which everyone can participate and prosper. Since October 2005, PolicyLink has been working in Louisiana to help ensure equitable redevelopment of the Gulf Coast region. For more information about Angela Glover Blackwell and PolicyLink, visit **www.policylink.org**.

Stephanie Robinson is the Founding President and CEO of The Jamestown Project, a national nonprofit, nonpartisan think/action tank dedicated to working to make real the American promise of democracy. She has worked for more than a decade in public and political spheres helping people, organizations, and communities to achieve social change. She served as the Chief Counsel to Senator Edward M. Kennedy (D-MA) in his role as Chair of the Senate Health, Education, Labor, and Pensions Committee. Currently, The Jamestown Project is bringing its experience, energy, and talents to the challenge of reforming the New Orleans criminal justice system for the 21st century. For more information about Stephanie Robinson and The Jamestown Project, visit **www.JamestownProject.org**.

Following is a conversation, moderated by Tavis Smiley, in which Blackwell and Robinson discuss the phenomenal reach and impact of the *Covenant with Black America*, why a manual to further inspire and guide action was needed, and for whom THE COVENANT *In Action* is designed to reach.

⌁

Tavis: Angela, let's start with a conversation about the *Covenant with Black America*. Why was that text so important to begin with?

Angela: The book catalyzed an extraordinary moment for black people, and indeed for the nation, because, in a simple, accessible, non-accusatory way, it jumpstarted a conversation within the black community about our individual and collective responsibilities for improving the state of Black America and simultaneously challenged the nation to find its better self and to truly build a vital democracy. The book not only provides important information—about health, education, criminal justice, etc.—it also presents that information with an action and a policy agenda that allows people to become engaged at the level most comfortable and accessible for them, thus considerably broadening the conversation and possibilities. The *Covenant with Black America* spoke to voters who wanted to be more informed about how to hold elected officials accountable, to the individual who wanted to take action, to faith institutions and community groups that wanted to sharpen and connect their agendas, and to leaders and elected officials wanting to be more accountable to the needs of Black America. It's not that the facts, action items, and policy fixes were not already out there; they were. The facts were pulled from other sources, the stories were about things that individuals and communities were already doing; the policy ideas were extracted from advocates who had been working in various fields. But by making it all simple, accessible, and then tied to a moment in time—C-SPAN's airing of the "State of the Black Union"—the facts, actions, and policies were catapulted into people's lives and a new phase of the movement for equity was launched. I think of the book as another "jewel in the crown" of the efforts of so many over the years that awed and inspired people to say: "Okay, we do have the knowledge. We do have the agenda. It's just a matter of us moving on it."

Tavis: So, Stephanie, you got involved at the point of THE COVENANT *In Action* text. But, tell me, why and how the *Covenant with Black America* impacted you.

Stephanie: I spent several years working as a Senior Advisor to a powerful United States senator. In that capacity, I talked "policy talk," recognizable only to a select few. Reading *The Covenant* reminded me how important it is to make sure that everybody—and I mean everybody in this democracy—truly understands what the terms of the debate are and can meaningfully participate in the decisions that impact their lives. Seeing the amazing response to *The Covenant* and everything that's a part of it—and the energy around it—affirmed, for me, how smart and gifted people are all around this country and what a thirst for knowledge and engagement black folk have. Whether young or old, they have a thirst for knowledge and truly want to be engaged. It further made me realize the role that I could play in being a part of what I think is an historic moment that you, Tavis, have been able to usher in, and that Black America has picked up on.

Tavis: Angela, before I get to what THE COVENANT *In Action* is, tell me why THE COVENANT *In Action* is the next step in this *Covenant* movement.

Angela: From observing the activities that black people began to pursue after reading and discussing *The Covenant*, I was struck by three things: people wanted to become engaged in action; the actions that most people pursued were helping activities in their communities and cities that immediately and directly impacted other people's lives; and that while a lot of the discussions surrounding *The Covenant* were about the systematic harm and disadvantage to black people that have resulted from past and continuing discrimination, there were not a lot of examples of advocacy efforts to address those issues. So, it seemed that the next step needed to both continue to inspire people to act close to home to improve conditions for blacks and to empower people to be effective advocates for broad systemic change. Our history in America has been one of helping each other; in fact, that has been what has enabled us to survive. So, it is thrilling to see us reviving and strengthening that tradition. But advocacy is also needed.

During the years that I have been engaged in social justice advocacy, I have observed that many people want to see and make change but don't know how to become engaged. It is often difficult to transition from the feeling of "I ought to do something" to actually being able to do something. As people read the book and talked about how to act to achieve *The Covenant* goals, it became obvious that we needed a bridge—from the discussion of the issues and an inspiration to act, to effective advocacy for change. To maintain momentum, people needed a glimpse of what others were doing, and they needed access to tools to be able to effectively fight for change. I find that people are often struggling with issues and challenges and doing the best that they can on their own; with a little help, sometimes that best can become enough. And so it seemed that the next step from the *Covenant with Black America* was to let people know what *The Covenant* had instigated and to help many more people work to improve the state of Black America by providing the tools and strategies for effective advocacy.

Tavis: So, Stephanie, that said, THE COVENANT *In Action* is designed to inspire people to take control of their own destiny, to fight for what they believe in, and to make a difference—which begs the question: What is an advocate?

Stephanie: I think that a person who represents, stands up for, champions the interest of another is the quintessential definition of an advocate. Many people think of an advocate as a lawyer or some professional. And that's true. But an advocate also can be a teacher, a student, a coach, a deacon in a church—any person who stands up for another, stands up on principle, and serves as the voice for people not otherwise heard. We have had advocates throughout our history, important people who have advocated on behalf of others. Ella Baker is someone who I think of as an extraordinary advocate. She represents the spirit of true inspiration and encouragement, in terms of empowering young people, and poor people, and women, and students—to lead their own movement and to be their own agents of change. I think that she did what we all want to do. She equipped people with the tools to express their wants, their needs, their desires—in a political arena that really, before now, was foreign to a lot of these groups. And I think that everyone can be an advocate by modeling, being a champion, and feeling that he or she has agency and voice, to be in charge of one's own destiny.

Tavis: Angela, tell me more about the public response to the first text the *Covenant with Black America*—which inspired this follow-up text.

Angela: Black people all over this country picked up the challenge of the *Covenant with Black America* and started doing something. There were book parties, where people just said, "Rather than read this book alone, let's read it with family and friends and talk about it together." When I talk to people who have gone to *Covenant* book parties, they have described how the event ended with discussion about an action agenda. People in elected positions, people who run government agencies started e-mailing me and saying, "We're going to pull together a work group. Could you come and talk to us and help us think about how, through our positions of power and influence, we can be more effective around this *Covenant* agenda?" Many community-based organizations and churches that were already active in the community saw *The Covenant* as a way to get people re-engaged, to be able to take the work that they were doing and to put it in the context of something that was part of a buzz all around the country. Many of these groups recast their work as a *Covenant* action. They found this gave their work more power and purpose. So, as I looked at what people have been doing, engaging their congregations, engaging their neighbors, and trying to figure out ways to engage youth, it became so clear that people did not see the *Covenant with Black America* as just a good read. They saw it as a mandate to act. And they were getting into the action on their own.

Tavis: Stephanie, talk to me about the importance—specifically in Black America—the importance of follow-through, developing an action agenda.

Stephanie: Follow-through is key. We can start, and we have begun many times, with a good idea—with a lot of passion, even, for the good idea; with a lot of information about a good idea. But a good idea is only as good as the people who take it to the next level and actually make it a reality. And it's important that we start looking at the coalitions that we can build in order to effect change. *The Covenant* puts an agenda out there. The next step here, THE COVENANT *In Action*, is part of *The Covenant* arsenal that equips people with the tools to be able to start operationalizing the agenda that we talk about. Other tools in this arsenal that Jamestown is producing are *The Covenant* Curriculum Manual & Study Guide; *The Covenant* for Children; and a new, foundational covenant about strengthening the family. These tools, made accessible through *The Covenant* website, permit us to start figuring out how to organize, how to agitate, how to connect with people, and how to do so in such a way that allows people to honor and respect each other, our history, and the stories of our past. When people are able to deeply connect in this way, they can lay out a blueprint to operate within the context that they find themselves in—whether it's a political context, whether it's a policy context, or whether it's a cultural context. For us to do something tangible with *The Covenant* agenda, it's important that we have a space and a place to do so. I personally thank you, Tavis, for creating this space with the "State of the Black Union," which allows us all a place and a time that will happen every year, where we will be able to have a conversation, as well as be able to get together and equip ourselves as a community, to figure out what our next steps are. THE COVENANT *In Action* and the entire *Covenant* arsenal that I speak of will help black folk of all ages from around the country to create blueprints for change. It will allow us to take all of the energy, rhetoric, and charisma that we have and couple those with a plan for follow-through so that this is not merely a moment in time, but a moment for the ages, so that it also becomes the legacy that is so important for Black America.

Angela: If I could just add a little bit to that. Over the years, I've been engaged in writing lots of briefs and reports on the very issues that are in the *Covenant with Black America*. And I daresay that probably even the best, most popular, and most accessible reports never reached more than 50,000 people, and that would have been a high point. The idea that we could take that same type of information—data, facts, policy recommendations—and make it accessible and put it out there and have a half-million people reading it and talking about it inspires me. And who knows how many people, really, have been informed by the *Covenant with Black America*? A half-million people purchased it, but how many copies were shared with others? How many people got the information and spirit of *The Covenant* just from participating in a discussion about it? How many people just picked up on the C-SPAN conversation and began their own deliberations? I suspect that easily millions of people are talking about the contents of the *Covenant with Black America*. And then to be able to help people understand that it's not just enough to talk about these issues with precision and passion, but you also need to be able to say that you are doing something to create change. So, THE COVENANT *In Action* is designed to equip people with the same level of rigor regarding advocacy that the *Covenant with Black America* provided regarding the challenges and solutions.

Tavis: Here's the exit question: First you, Stephanie, and you, Angela, you have the last word—what is the hope in producing this document? And, who in fact, should read THE COVENANT *In Action*?

Stephanie: The hope in producing THE COVENANT *In Action* is to give voice and agency to Black America, to allow black Americans an opportunity to put their knowledge, their talents, their voice, and their passion forward. And, as Angela started to say, I think that creating this opportunity that allows us to have an organizing framework that connects people to something larger than their individual selves, their individual families, or their individual communities is really the hope for what we want to do. It's a hope of giving voice and agency to black folk so that they can make real the promises of American democracy. It's helping America live up to its democratic aspirations.

Who should read this manual? I would venture to say that everyone should read this manual—just as everyone should read the *Covenant with Black America*. These books are the beginning of the building of a movement that is not just about Black America. Quite frankly, this is about all Americans in our democracy. We really want young people to read this book; that's important to us. In fact we have young advocates who've written essays in this book. Through their own words and their own stories, they inspire their peers and others to act. We want older people to read this book. We want older, more seasoned advocates to read this book so that they can be reinvigorated and inspired. So in the end, this book is for all Americans who care about justice, fairness, and equality.

Tavis: Angela?

Angela: Without question, when you make Black America better, you make *all* of America better, because when you authentically address the problems of those who suffer most visibly, you end up removing obstacles and barriers for many who were suffering in silence or invisibly. Ending slavery unleashed the economic potential of this country; the civil rights movement emboldened women and other racial and ethnic minorities to stand up for their rights, and the country reaped the benefits of their contributions. And now, addressing the lingering negative consequences of historical and continuing discrimination (which is really what was revealed in the *Covenant with Black America*) will secure democracy into the 21st century. But achieving this goal will require advocacy on the part of a lot of people, and not just black people. There's really nothing in THE COVENANT *In Action* that's limited to black people. Anybody who cares about justice and inclusion can pick up this manuscript and use the tools and strategies to advance justice. So, I agree with Stephanie that this is a book for everybody because the hope is for everybody. We need a change in this country. In fact, we need a change in the world. To address societal inequities, that change must come from a moral place. The people who have read the *Covenant with Black America* and who have become outraged by the facts can now pick up this COVENANT *In Action* and feel equipped to begin making a difference. They are the ones who are going to cause change, in the nation and in the world, to happen.

But there's one other thing: to sustain this change over time, people have to own *The Covenant* movement as their own. And I think that's the thing I love most about the *Covenant with Black America*: there is no *"The Covenant"* organization. *The Covenant* is public information for people to be able to take and act upon in their own names, in the names of their organizations, consistent with *The Covenant's* aspirations and values, to make a difference in this world, for black people, for all people. To be sustained, *The Covenant* movement has to live beyond PolicyLink and The Jamestown Project and even The Smiley Group. It has to live broadly, across society, among those people who say, "I have an obligation to act on this knowledge and use the best tools and strategies to make and secure a better future."

THE COVENANT *In Action:*
What Individuals and
Communities Are Doing

As copies of the *Covenant with Black America* were flying off of bookshelves, people eagerly began to talk with friends, coworkers, and neighbors about how they could organize around changing their lives and communities. The book sparked nationwide action, and thousands of African Americans of all ages, professions, and persuasions created challenging initiatives to advance *The Covenant* goals. There have been far too many activities to present them all in great detail; thousands of individuals and hundreds of organizations have become engaged, including: The Links, Inc., who are using *The Covenant* as a guide to train their young members on how to be active in their communities; Delta Sigma Theta Sorority, Inc., and Kappa Alpha Psi Fraternity, Inc., who adopted specific *Covenants* most relevant to their chapters all over the country; numerous cities that continue to hold town hall meetings; and high schools and colleges that have included *The Covenant* in their curriculums. The illustrative efforts, highlighted in the following pages, are part of a massive collective struggle to make Black America better.

Since the movement has just taken off, the programs presented are very promising works in progress. Significant and lasting change is not made overnight, and we are eager to see the progress they will have made a year from now. For any individuals, organizations, or church groups trying to organize around *The Covenant* goals, we hope these efforts that have been set into motion will offer you guidance and inspiration.

The Value of Mass Mobilization: Renewing the Voting Rights Act

Just five months after the *Covenant with Black America* was released, a broad coalition of civil rights organizations came together to fight successfully for the renewal of the Voting Rights Act. Yet it was the thousands of individuals bombarding their senators' offices with their phone calls, showing their faces, and lobbying on Capitol Hill who were responsible for persuading elected officials to reauthorize this vital legislation. Their collective action represented a milestone, since renewing the Voting Rights Act was one of *The Covenant* goals. Once again, mass grassroots mobilization affirmed the power of individual and collective voice.

During July 2006, advocates for reauthorizing the Voting Rights Act were met with opposition from several members of the U.S. Congress. Undaunted, they generated over 15,000 calls to various senatorial offices for more than a week and a half. Then on the Monday before the vote, the people proved their power. One opposing senator's phones were shut down because of the volume of calls. In addition, a coalition of grassroots organizations encouraged individuals to file over 100,000 reauthorization petitions.

During his nationally syndicated *Morning Show*, Tom Joyner joined in the efforts by alerting his radio audience to the dire situation and encouraging them to call their senators right away. Thousands did just that, demanding their lawmakers to support the renewal.

In a final push, more than 2,000 members of the NAACP—who were in town for their national convention, where President George W. Bush for the first time had accepted their invitation to speak—marched up to Capitol Hill. These determined individuals, without great wealth or well-known names and faces, "because of the clarity of their message, the sincerity of their view, and their willingness to walk the halls of Congress ultimately succeeded," stated Wade Henderson, Executive Director of the Leadership Conference on Civil Rights. "When the senators saw the presence of that many black people on Capitol Hill," Henderson recalled, "it altered the psychology of members of the Senate and House. They were actually moved by the sheer numbers and magnitude of the effort."

On July 20, 2006, the Senate Judiciary Committee voted in favor of reauthorizing the Voting Rights Act. That same day, President Bush addressed the NAACP and spoke adamantly of his support of the Act. Seven days later, he signed the bill, renewing the 1965 Voting Rights Act for another 25 years.

A profound lesson was learned from this process and must be applied to all of our struggles: The power of a single individual, when combined with many, creates a mighty force.

Parties with a Purpose

To celebrate the inspirational and historic success of the *Covenant with Black America* and to continue the book's dialogue, Tavis Smiley invited the public to join in hosting *Covenant* book parties nationwide May 19–21, 2006, as part of *The Covenant* Conversation & Celebration Weekend. Smiley said, "To coin a popular phrase, 'it's a party with a purpose' . . . [T]his weekend celebration is an opportunity for everyone who cares about this movement and moment in history to mark this achievement together."

Nearly 250 parties attended by thousands of guests were held in 30 states. As Kyla Browning, a member of Zora's Daughters book club in Houston, Texas, reflected on *The Covenant* dialogue she participated in, she was "deeply moved by the idea of so many beautiful black people thinking, sharing, and strategizing about how to live healthier, safer, and more prosperous lives, at the same moment in time." She continued, "Even though we were separated by distance, it was as if there was a common thread that touched each of us and kept us connected with one mind and one heart that day."

Ten hosts were randomly selected to receive calls during their events from *Covenant* contributors, including Congresswoman Sheila Jackson Lee of Texas; Angela Glover Blackwell, Founder and CEO of PolicyLink; Iyanla Vanzant, author and spiritual life counselor; Nikki Giovanni, author and professor, Virginia Tech; Sonia Sanchez, poet, activist, and educator; and Tom Joyner, the nationally syndicated radio host. As winner of the grand prize, Pamela Johnson's *Covenant* celebration in Upper Marlboro, MD, included guests Cornel West, professor of religion, Princeton University; and Tavis Smiley. Johnson says she took the first step to keeping the spirit of *The Covenant* alive by providing each of her guests with "a commitment bag . . . that contained items to reiterate the importance of sustaining black businesses, attending or supporting Historically Black Colleges and Universities, and promoting education."

When it came to creativity, the style of the parties ran the gamut—from a U.S. military black-tie event to a fish fry; from a tea party to a good old-fashioned read-aloud; from a book club to a family meeting; from an intimate dinner party to a pamper party with manicures and massages; and from an investment party to a panel of youth who presented their *Covenant* analysis to their elders. One of the unique *Covenant* celebrations was a "Bridal and Enlightenment Shower" held over a weekend getaway in Fort Lauderdale, FL. Jacqueline Suggs of Virginia was one of the event's coordinators, who explained that while the shower was already planned, when she heard Smiley's invitation, "It seemed natural for six professional black women interested in bettering their race and working towards a safer world for children to set aside a portion of the weekend to discuss *The Covenant* agenda." The lasting message for Suggs and her friends was that we must "always be cognizant of the issues in the book, because they don't end there; those concerns are actually the issues in our lives and our communities. It is always possible to attend to our spiritual, financial, emotional, and healthful well-being." As we move further away from *The Covenant* Conversation & Celebration Weekend, it is our hope that everyone who attended a party weekend continues to make time to take action.

For Lynnette Yankson of the 100 Buddhists Book Club in Atlanta, GA, the energy surrounding *The Covenant* movement stimulated her to get involved. The members of her club felt compelled to address health, education, and criminal and environmental justice. Every Sunday since its *Covenant* party, the health committee has met for an early dinner and discussion about living healthy lives. Its members are proponents of the "live food lifestyle" and eat at Lov'n It Live organic and vegan restaurant weekly. Yankson believes that this has become a support group for people transitioning to a diet of organic living (raw) and vegan cuisine and plans to use *The Covenant* as a guide to raise others' awareness of critical health issues.

Concerned and conscientious black Americans of all ages participated in *The Covenant* Conversation & Celebration Weekend. The Butterfly Brigade, a group of senior women, was founded during the gathering hosted by Elaine T. Jones of Hampton, VA. In her words, they "came together with expertise, information, and knowledge that only come through years of education, experience, and trotting on life's path." Interestingly, the majority of the group was most interested in dissecting Covenant III: "Correcting the System of Unequal Justice" above all others. As mothers and grandmothers, they felt that it was particularly urgent to begin to repair this unbalanced institution so as not to continue to lose so many of our children. By the end of the productive and eye-opening day, the women decided to call themselves "The Butterfly Brigade" because "whereas the beautiful little butterfly flaps its wings and causes the 'Butterfly Effect,' each of our small, daily actions of intent can cause a positive change in the social atmosphere," Jones stated.

The Covenant Celebrations left individuals more enlightened, aware, and equipped to begin to help make Black America better. If we take the first step at home and in our own lives, then we can share our knowledge with friends, families, and, in time, the rest of the world.

Hurricanes Katrina, Rita, and the *Covenant with Black America*

A disaster recovery manager, an advisor to the governor, and a top researcher in higher education were among the group of travelers on a journey that began with a little road trip to Texas. In the winter of 2006, these young African-American professionals from Louisiana traveled to Houston to attend the "State of the Black Union." Each had followed this annual event on C-SPAN and welcomed the positive and empowering focus of the meeting that turned the dialogue from a discussion of problems affecting African Americans to solutions. "It is an understatement to say that we were excited to read *The Covenant* and, upon our return, proceeded to spread the message of *The Covenant*, which urged African Americans to work to make 'America as good as its promise,'" stated Dominique Duval-Diop, Policy and Reporting Manager, Disaster Recovery Unit, Office of Community Development, State of Louisiana.

This message changed the way that Duval-Diop and her colleagues—James Gilmore, Vice President, Louisiana Housing Finance Authority (formerly Social Services), Housing Advisor to the Governor of Louisiana; Adren Wilson, Assistant Secretary, Department of Social Services, State of Louisiana; Hamady Diop, Research Faculty, LSU Sea Grant; Joe Lott, Postdoctoral Fellow, University of Texas – Austin; and Kimberly Levy, Constituent Services, Governor's Office, State of Louisiana—viewed their personal power and the potential of their positions of leadership in the state. "We took this message to heart and were inspired in a personal way to work to harness our collective power and networks to bring about meaningful change for citizens in our state and ultimately in the world."

A *Covenant* group was soon developed, and it brought in other key young African-American leaders to brainstorm how they could collectively work to better the lives of the most disadvantaged. Although they "had collaborated in the past, this time the collaboration was more solid and focused," Duval-Diop observed.

To reverse the impact of Hurricanes Katrina and Rita, the Louisiana team endeavored to connect two separate initiatives (the new statewide Louisiana VISTA program and the existing Solutions to Poverty community coalitions) to broaden the impact of both. It sought to ensure that recovery programs funded through $10.4 billion of supplemental Community Development Block Grants would facilitate, not impede, the individual recovery and neighborhood rebuilding process. Essentially, "we strengthened and focused what had primarily been an informal social network to a network empowered to actively seek better outcomes for the displaced people of Louisiana and ultimately for the entire state," Duval-Diop continued.

Several of the Louisiana residents also personally pledged to have an individual impact outside of their jobs. One participated in a Habitat for Humanity project to build houses for hurricane evacuees; others have reached out to similar progressive groups, creating a multiplier effect. They believe that "there is no limit to the good that we can do collectively and individually. The *Covenant with Black America* allowed us to focus our individual voices to raise them in a unified clamor demanding change," Duval-Diop concluded.

NFBPA and *The Covenant*

Members of the National Forum for Black Public Administrators (NFBPA) have spent the past several months doing their *Covenant with Black America* homework. Sharon Ofuani, president of the Council of Presidents, "ran out and got the book after watching the 'State of the Black Union.'" The timing was ideal for her because as the incoming chief executive, she decided to propose that the organization's chapters officially support *The Covenant* agenda as their new project.

NFBPA is the principal and most progressive organization dedicated to the advancement of black public leadership in local and state governments. An independent, nonpartisan, 501(c)(3) nonprofit organization founded in 1983, it has established a national reputation for designing and implementing quality leadership development initiatives of unparalleled success. Its 2,500-plus members manage public programs and agencies in more than 350 jurisdictions nationwide. Thirty-nine chapters support the growth of the organization at the local level.

The organization's mission is threefold, as explained by NFBPA National President Harry Jones: "to increase the number of African Americans appointed to executive positions in municipal, county, and state governments; to enhance the managerial capacity of African-American administrators in public service agencies; and to groom younger, emerging black administrators for the challenges they will face as public-service executives addressing the vital and multifaceted needs of urban, suburban, and rural America."

Because public policy is such an integral part of public administration, "*The Covenant* presented an excellent opportunity to be the guide for helping us coordinate some of our efforts," Ofuani noted. "Certainly, as *The Covenant* is all about public policy, it's a natural fit for our chapters in NFBPA to connect with the intent and spirit of *The Covenant.*"

NFBPA chapter presidents and members attended numerous town hall meetings; others were extremely supportive, so much so that when Ofuani proposed adopting *The Covenant* agenda as its new project, the Council of Presidents unanimously voted its approval.

As evidence of their support and interest, John Saunders, Executive Director of NFBPA, and Ofuani invited PolicyLink CEO Angela

Glover Blackwell to speak to their Board of Directors, National Corporate Advisory Council, Council of Presidents, and members of various Board committees at their quarterly leadership conference in Wichita, Kansas. She provided an overview of the book and offered guidance about how NFBPA might embrace *The Covenant*. As a result, they are proposing that the national board come up with an official position on how to most effectively support *The Covenant* movement.

According to National President Jones, NFBPA is eager to explore how to promote the goals of the *Covenant with Black America* because it sees the document as "a blueprint for civic activities to help black people live healthier, safer, and more prosperous lives."

Concord Baptist Church and the *CWBA*

At the second stop on the inspirational *Covenant with Black America* tour, the streets surrounding Concord Baptist Church in Brooklyn's Bedford-Stuyvesant neighborhood were buzzing with anticipation. By subway, bus, car, and foot, thousands of New Yorkers converged on the church to join a groundbreaking national discussion on an African-American policy agenda for economic and social equity. Parents, children, and groups of friends overflowed the sanctuary, filling the church's aisles, balcony, and basement. For Rev. Gary Simpson, this was just the beginning of his ceaseless commitment to furthering *The Covenant* goals.

Concord's town hall meeting sparked an ongoing stream of events organized around the principles and solutions presented in *The Covenant*. Rev. Simpson developed a 10-week *Covenant* Sermon Series in which he provided a biblical framework for each *Covenant* goal. In the meantime, a group of community activists, including Rev. Simpson, had begun to plan the Black Brooklyn Empowerment Convention (BBEC), an all-day dialogue held in June 2006 with close to 3,000 citizens.

The question of whether or not any of the 10 *Covenants* are biblically based was raised a number of times—from an interview on Christian radio to the skepticism of other pastors and to the curiosity of congregants. To enlighten Concord's members, Rev. Simpson spent days connecting chapter and verse to each tenet of *The Covenant* agenda.

He believed it was crucial to provide convincing evidence of why "this is a conversation that Christian people need to be in on, and why [we] can't opt out of a dialogue that is at the heart of our identity." His hope was that once he presented the context and "demonstrated why this matters to God," his congregants would take charge of their lives and the ills in their community.

The next step was the Black Brooklyn Empowerment Convention, whose mission was "to bring together African-American, Caribbean, African, and Afro-Latino ethnicities, nationalities, communities, constituencies, and diverse socioeconomic classes, genders, age groups, and their leaders to discuss, define, and agree upon a collective Black Policy Agenda that encompasses our critical issues and concerns. This common agenda will then be advocated by convention participants, broader constituencies, and leadership and used as a yardstick by which to hold leadership accountable for representing our interests and empowering our communities."

One of the convention chairmen—New York City Council Member Al Vann, a Bedford-Stuyvesant native—planned a similar convention 26 years ago in Brooklyn; Rev. Simpson termed him the "spiritual godfather of the movement." Over the course of an eight-hour program, Vann, Rev. Simpson, and several others planned sessions addressing: Health & Human Services, Housing & Economic Development, Education, Criminal Justice & Public Safety, the Judicial System, Civic Engagement & Voting Rights, Black Culture & Values, and International Affairs & Immigration. The daylong conference covered suggestions for action and policy recommendations, much like the *Covenant with Black America* and Concord's own town hall meeting. Workshop presenters developed detailed steps anyone can take to create change in his or her community, including "create Health Empowerment Zones to implement strategies to increase the number of black and culturally sensitive medical doctors, health professionals, and caregivers in our community; assist teachers and administrators to better understand the home and school culture and language of students of African and Caribbean descent and how they can be effectively used to engage students in meaningful learning; and monitor police officers and prosecution practices of Brooklyn's District Attorneys by black elected officials and activists." Participants were also encouraged to contribute and devise their own policy recommendations and suggestions for individuals.

Brooklyn is a particularly unique city, home to a million black people of various persuasions—the largest black diaspora community in the world.[1] Rev. Simpson acknowledged that "both Marcus Garvey and Adam Clayton Powell" were in the meeting, and with such a varied mix of ideologies and philosophies, there was an initial concern that folks would not be able to overcome their differences. "The day was blessed," Rev. Simpson observed; and even though everyone came together carrying great pain and frustration, people listened to one another.

Much to Rev. Simpson's dismay, the one noticeably absent segment of Brooklyn's population was the youth. Organizers recognized that they must figure out how to capture the imagination of young people and struggled to pull them in. In Bedford-Stuyvesant alone, there are 40,000 people under the age of 18. Because it has "become increasingly more difficult to bridge the generational gap," Rev. Simpson suggested that "creating an agenda that is pursued by and for young people and generations to come is not only the challenge of the Black Brooklyn Empowerment Project, but also of our time." When a conference attendee raised the question of why the civil rights movement was so intergenerational, the response was "at the time, second, third, and fourth graders were going to jail and being required, coaxed, forced, and cajoled by parents, teachers, and ministers to go to sit-ins and boycott segregated schools for the sake of the movement." This does not apply today, but the 3,000 conference participants set out to identify and clearly define the equivalent actions for African-American youth in 2006 and beyond.

Through dialogue around the goals of the *Covenant with Black America*, residents of Bedford-Stuyvesant witnessed how many intelligent, informed, and savvy doctors and teachers, laborers and mothers, and fathers and preachers have plans they had not heard. Rev. Simpson was one of the many who left the convention feeling "incredibly proud to be black in Brooklyn that day."

BBEC attendees have continued to meet on Saturdays to further develop specific plans of action around the issues. Rev. Simpson believes that their greatest success is the "potential to last while so many things we do in the black community are event oriented. We spend

---

[1] This statistic and other quoted information in this article were extrapolated from a handout distributed at the Black Brooklyn Empowerment Convention.

our time talking about 'were you there?' But we have begun to ask: 'What are you doing now?' 'How are you keeping *The Covenant* rolling?' African Americans must make a lifestyle change; it would be a big shift if we just adjusted the way we talk to each other, to simply say 'brother and sister'—that is a revolution in the making."

Peoria Embraces *The Covenant*

A small but powerful team of active citizens and educators, brought together by Lori Brown of the Disproportionate Minority Confinement Children's Home Association of Illinois, spearheaded Peoria's *Covenant* efforts. After watching "The State of the Black Union" on C-SPAN in February 2006, Brown downloaded *The Covenant* toolkit and invited several friends and colleagues to help her organize a town hall meeting. The team was drawn to the project because "it talked very specifically about what individuals can do, and often times [we] hear about mass movements but don't internalize their messages because we don't understand how to get involved."

Brown realized that a long-time friend, James Bell, had not only written the introductory essay for Covenant III: "Correcting the System of Unequal Justice," but he was also scheduled to speak at a conference on juvenile justice in Peoria. She recalls that "this was divine intervention from the beginning; everything just fell into place."

Considering that Peoria is 25 percent black with a population of close to 115,000 and a median household income of about $37,000 a year, the planning team decided to focus on the three *Covenants* most relevant to what has consistently plagued the city: Education, Criminal Justice, and Economic Prosperity. Bell, head of the Haywood Burns Institute; Dr. Herschel Hannah, Assistant Superintendent, Peoria Public Schools; Sharon Desmoulin-Kherat, principal, Whittier Primary School; Bashir Ali, Workforce Development Director, Workforce Network; and Carlton Adams, General Manager, CAT Product Manufacturing Division were invited to speak on their respective specialties to help lay the groundwork for the plan of action.

Two of the planning team organizers are staff members at Bradley University, where the Black Student Union annually hosts a "Day of Dialogue." The Peoria town hall planning committee agreed to link with it—an established group that hosts an annual event—to ensure *The Covenant* Conversation's longevity.

When the time came to encourage folks to attend the town hall meeting, the organizers were unapologetic about talking just to African Americans as it was a "conversation about us, and we can have it better with just us in the room," Brown pointed out. *The Covenant* reminds us that we need to take responsibility for our lives and make some different choices; it is often most effective to speak to one another candidly within our own communities.

By e-mail, telephone, and word of mouth, Brown and her colleagues reached out to nearly every African American they knew—through churches, local organizations, schools, fraternities, sororities, friends, and family. More than 1,100 people attended the town hall meeting—a great turnout, according to Brown, because Peoria does not have a strong history of community activism.

From the town hall meeting, the *Covenant with Black America* Study Circles were born. The Study Circles program is a tool to foster public dialogue and community change. Small groups, led by an impartial facilitator who helps manage the conversation, share personal perspectives, openly explore problems and their possible solutions, and ultimately create plans for action and change.

To develop an organized and a formal strategy that folks would remain committed to, organizers were officially trained in the Study Circles method. Eighty-five of those who attended the town hall meeting signed up for one of three Study Circles and reunited four months later to attack the complex issues of equity in public education, criminal justice, and economic prosperity. This was the first of four gatherings leading to an all-inclusive meeting where each individual Study Circle came together to share ideas, designate specific roles, and create a concrete action plan to better the black community in Peoria.

The residents, ranging in age from their early 20s to their late 60s, have already devised a few tangible solutions, including introducing a basic economics program in middle and high schools that addresses the value of a dollar, the importance of a savings account, and how to balance a checkbook. It demands that educators support the program. Participants also emphasize supporting black businesses in ways large and small, such as buying a subscription to the local black newspaper. They note that if friends or family members view patronizing only black-owned businesses as racist, they should respond that "it is not about bigotry, it is about black love, and if we are going to talk about wanting our brothers and sisters to prosper, we must actively support them."

Lori Brown acknowledges that the most anticipated challenge of the *Covenant with Black America* efforts in Peoria is keeping people involved and interested. Her team has asked for a substantial commitment from people who lead very busy lives, but it hangs on to the hope that "if we can individually recognize our power and our strength, just think of what we can do collectively." Brown added, "We have tried before, but having *The Covenant* as our motivator and guide might just be what is different this time."

San Francisco and *The Covenant*

When the *Covenant with Black America* was still in its early production stages, Mayor Gavin Newsom of San Francisco and his staff were already planning their town hall meeting. Their immediate commitment to promoting the goals of *The Covenant* and introducing their citizens to activism was particularly unique, as they had not even seen the book and were simply acting on the belief that *The Covenant* would be the guide residents could use to begin to turn their lives around. The San Francisco event was the last stop on the first leg of *The Covenant* town hall meeting tour in 2006, and the mayor's office took the initiative to coordinate every aspect of the forum on its own, which resulted in a remarkably well-attended, informative, and productive foundation for many progressive initiatives to come.

Twelve-hundred African Americans of all ages participated in the dialogue; overflow rooms were filled to capacity and beyond—some folks had to be turned away. While some initiatives such as *Communities of Opportunity*—"a truly innovative, place-based strategy of renewal that is being developed through a partnership of community residents, government officials, community leaders, and philanthropic organizations," which had a substantive link to *The Covenant*—were already in progress, many other ideas resulted from the event, where citizens immediately adopted *The Covenant*. Residents were energized by the conversation and instantly supported one another in developing and moving on uncompromising agendas. "We were able to use *The Covenant* as a point of departure for a lot of progressive activity," pointed out Fred Blackwell, the Co-Director of the Mayor's Office of Community Development. The results of the town hall meeting are astonishing and inspirational to anyone attempting to promote a plan for change.

The first of these programs, a spoken-word competition for young people, took place a few months after the event. Thirty residents of San Francisco's "Four Corners" housing development wrote about the pressing issues in their community and shared them, along with other personal poetry. This was an outlet for young men and women ages 17–30 to use their creative voice to begin to effect change in their own communities. Dwayne Jones, Co-Director of the Mayor's Office of Community Development, was responsible for tapping into the strength of many of these young African Americans; through lyrical artistry, a tool with which they could vent and be heard, their sense of duty was awakened, deeply engaging them in the city-wide effort to better the black community. Round two was planned for January of 2007, with the four winners of the competition traveling to Jamestown to participate in the 2007 "State of the Black Union." Co-Director Jones said the poets "like the fact that they are a part of a national movement that will connect them to others with similar motives and aspirations."

San Francisco's *Covenant* team targeted youth from the beginning of this movement and thought that the best way to spark their interest was to invest in a vehicle that would quickly draw them in without their even realizing they were learning in the process. A little over a thousand dollars worth of tickets to a concert by R&B singer Chris Brown provided a platform to teach people about the goals of the *Covenant with Black America* and to have fun while uniting with one another around common issues. One Saturday in June, residents of Alice Griffith, West Point, Oakdale, and Sunnydale housing developments had to call in and either recite the 10 *Covenants* or the principles of *Communities of Opportunity*. More than 225 residents called; while they were on hold, they heard a prerecorded message about *The Covenant*. This tactic immediately spread awareness, got them excited, and left them wondering: "How do I join? When is the next contest?" While they were initially waiting for the next contest, soon they were excited about doing work to further *The Covenant* agenda. Jones noticed that "it became less about the tickets and more about the impact they were having with their brothers and sisters on their community."

The next step in engaging San Francisco's youth was to go door to door and ask residents questions to gauge their interest in different *Covenant* topics. Staff offered residents choices of issues and three different types of action to choose from; for example, if they selected education, they could join the PTA, advocate at the school board, or tutor children. From this, the city's *Covenant* Clubs were born. Participants organized by housing development, met on a regular basis, and began by setting their agenda. As this book goes to press, 270 young people are involved, in 30 different clubs—usually 10 per development—each working on a specific *Covenant*. Each division of the clubs is responsible for recruiting new members from their respective developments.

Because there was not a theme that did not correlate with some subset of the community, the clubs chose to attack all 10 issues. The general idea, Jones noted, was that "if [we] fixed 'this,' other things would work much easier." The clubs do some overlapping work, and some, such as the Environmental Justice and Health groups, connect on issues including asthma and lead poisoning.

The clubs have recently enrolled in programs designed via *Communities of Opportunity* that should mitigate *The Covenant* issues they are trying to address. The Education *Covenant* Clubs have recruited 100 youth from each development for a city-sponsored academic program, *T-Tens,* based on W.E.B. Du Bois's "talented tenth," to be tracked to be doctors, lawyers, scientists, and teachers—the professionals they believe are necessary to create a stable and thriving community. The students start in the fifth grade; the clubs hope to identify corporations that would pay the college tuition for participating students upon their graduation from high school.

Some of the most remarkable changes have taken place around "Bridging the Digital Divide." San Francisco, in partnership with the Full Circle Fund, One Economy, and IMHETEP TEKH, already had an initiative in the works to "wi-fi"—or wire—the entire city so that all residents would have free, high-speed, broadband Internet access; in an unexpected turn, the energy around *The Covenant* allowed the partnership to push to wire low-income and black communities first and to use that housing development as a model for the rest of the city.

Two-hundred-fifty units in one of the public housing developments were connected, with the wi-fi radius covering the school next door to it; another 300 homes outside of the development were also wired. Each household was provided a desktop computer in addition to the Internet access. Staff has used the web to communicate with residents about credit and financial resources, GED preparation, continuing education, and other things they need to live healthy prosperous lives.

Using technology to diminish poverty has yielded many exciting results. The San Francisco *Covenant* website was designed by youth in the Technology *Covenant* Clubs who were charged with identifying *Covenant* action pieces that were happening in their neighborhoods and then using an instructional program to develop and maintain the site. Their training is ongoing, and the web is being updated regularly. According to Co-Director Jones, "This was a scenario where folks read that chapter and really pushed the initiative that was already in motion. It pulled out a platform for us to marshal the resources in a more aggressive way."

The Covenant Clubs were not the only projects spurred by the town hall meeting. A number of attendees were interested in follow-up organizing. The African-American Action Network, a newly formed organization, partnered with Mayor Newsom's office to host the city's Health Summit in December 2006.

The summit's opening plenary panel focused on health disparities in the African-American community. Next were three workshops presented by age—young people, adults, and seniors—based on the premise that health issues differ by age group. Ten concurrent workshops followed that addressed asthma, cardiovascular disease, violence, and prostate and breast cancer. Participants learned from experts in the field about health risks and how to deal with them. Another highlight was a farmer's market that featured products from African-American farmers in California's Central Valley.

The day closed with a discussion on the recent passing of the mayor's Universal Healthcare Plan. Attendees were instructed on the plan's enrollment and its benefits. According to Fred Blackwell, they wanted the "event to establish some sort of infrastructure for action" and to serve as a "jumping-off point for folks to take action on a health improvement agenda for African Americans."

San Francisco has made remarkable advancements, and Jones credits the mayor for being involved in every step of *The Covenant* movement. According to Jones, the mayor charged him, his Co-Director, and their team "with making sure that each piece was a solid example of community transformation." The mayor not only immediately recognized the power of youth, but he also had ideas on how best to mobilize them.

One of the greatest strengths of San Francisco's *Covenant* effort is its ability to interest young people in bettering their communities and to keep them engaged while also essentially running the programs themselves. Job training organizations and initiatives are intimately tied to *The Covenant* ideals. Youth who are engaged become employed or end up in the pipeline to gain employment as a result of their participation. Co-Director Jones has noticed that "the number-one issue for the disconnect of youth is that no one is talking to them in language that they need to hear, which is 'where can I get some money so that I can think about what I'm going to do for the future?'" Three main reasons motivate young folks to participate in *The Covenant* Clubs: freedom of expression, access to opportunities, and technology training. As one young woman put it, "If we are either responsible for 90 percent of the issues or impacted disproportionately, why isn't there a mechanism for us to be part of the solution?" The youthful residents of San Francisco's housing developments *are* part of the solution, having embraced *The Covenant* and its goals as their own.

A Philanthropic *Covenant with Black America*

In working to advance the goals of *The Covenant*, philanthropy can be considered as either part of the problem or part of the solution. The National Center for Black Philanthropy, Inc. (NCFBP), has adopted the theme of "Philanthropy and the *Covenant with Black America*" for its sixth annual national conference, set for June 2007 in Washington, DC. As Rodney M. Jackson, President and CEO, read the *Covenant with Black America*, he realized it did not talk about philanthropy, which led him to "wonder how we plan to change our communities without substantial funding and resources."

The 500 conference participants will examine: how to increase overall funding in the black community; models of strategic partnerships that now exist between funders and the black community or that need to be developed; how we can increase our own giving; and how nonprofit organizations serving the black community can become more effective in addressing the issues in *The Covenant*. Through dialogue and workshops, NCFBP organizers hope to "develop common solutions and strategies that demonstrate how African-American philanthropy in the areas of individual giving, grant-making, fundraising, and faith-based philanthropy can address the various social and economic problems that continue to afflict black people today."

Prior to the conference, NCFBP plans to draft "A Philanthropic *Covenant with Black America"* that will cover strengthening black communities through personal philanthropy, grant-making, and churches and religious institutions, as well as the role that youth and young professionals play in the success of philanthropy. It will begin this project by interviewing "fifty of the most prominent individuals associated with black philanthropy in order to gain wisdom and recommendations," Jackson stated. The first draft of the Philanthropy *Covenant* will be presented to the conference attendees as the basis for discussion and debate, allowing for a collective and transparent development and writing process. The document will then be finalized, with a goal of having A Philanthropic *Covenant with Black America* readily available at bookstores nationwide.

According to the National Center for Black Philanthropy, in terms of donating money, African Americans are among the most generous people in the country, giving close to $11 billion in 2004—just $2 billion less than all of the corporations in the United States combined gave in that same year. Jackson continued that the "goal is to start a philanthropic revolution in response to the issues raised in the *Covenant with Black America* so that we will have the resources defined as 'time, talent, and treasure' to make an impact in our own world. We must harness the energy in our community and get our own folks mobilized."

For more information about the National Center for Black Philanthropy, Inc., and its 2007 national conference, visit **www.ncfbp.net**.

THE COVENANT *In Action:*
Voices of Black America's
Young Activists

The *Covenant with Black America* has clearly struck a responsive chord with black people from many walks of life. We know that the future will depend on young people becoming active, getting engaged, and demanding that America lives up to its promises. Many of the changes we will set in motion will likely take effect over the course of many years; future generations will benefit from our efforts. Therefore, youth must be among the leaders of *The Covenant* movement. The experiences of the young people engaged in advancing *The Covenant* goals in San Francisco and Louisiana described in the last section are inspiring; we *must* find ways to tap into the interests and creativity of many more youth if we are to succeed.

More and more young people are organizing on their own, sharing their knowledge and skills with great compassion. They developed their own "COVENANTS *In Action*." As with the youth who are finding their leadership legs through *The Covenant*, these extraordinary young adults typify and ensure the commitment, growth, and future of *The Covenant* movement. A cross-sampling of their stories follows.

Helping the Homeless Through NAPS[2]

In 1978, a group of black students at Oakwood College, an histori-cally black college in Huntsville, Alabama, saw some homeless people huddled under a bridge and decided to feed them. Their effort even-tually led to the formation of the National Association for the Pre-vention of Starvation, or NAPS, a 501(c)(3) nonprofit volunteer relief organization. Its mission: to alleviate hunger, poverty, and disease; and to improve education and food security among suffering people, both nationally and internationally, regardless of race, religion, socio-economic status, or nationality. The organization provides humani-tarian aid and educational support in the areas of emergency relief, skilled volunteers, healthcare professionals, agricultural technology, and social and spiritual comfort. NAPS operates independently of all governmental, institutional, or political influences.

NAPS has visited various juvenile detention centers and prisons in some of the toughest cities in America, motivating young men and women to better themselves and to become leaders of tomor-row. NAPS seeks to spread the importance of community involvement through service and to let youth know that they have the resilience to make change and to impact our world today. There is nothing more rewarding than to see children helping children; when a child hands a homeless person a bowl of food or article of clothing, they are both blessed. Such is the service-oriented spirit of NAPS.

NAPS has engaged in feeding and humanitarian programs in Cali-fornia, New York, Miami, Ethiopia, Zambia, and Haiti, among other locales. It has fed over a half-million people during the past 18 years and has touched countless other lives through its educational and mentoring programs.

Several NAPS volunteers annually dedicate a year of service to hu-manity in what they refer to as a "Year of Dedication" (YOD). Volun-teers for the present YOD have traveled to Boston, Connecticut, New

---

[2] This essay was authored by Dr. Anthony D. Paul, President of NAPS, who is also the Chair and a Professor of the Department of Biological Sciences at Oakwood College. He has been published in each of the following research and development specialization disciplines: chemistry, botany, physiology, and neuroscience. He has received the National Honor for Leadership in Premedical Education from The Global Initiative for Telemedicine, Inc., and The Thomas and Violet Zappara Excellence in Teaching Award, Office of Education, North America Division. He is a member of the American Institute of Biological Sciences and the American Association for the Advancement of Science.

York, and Miami, visiting schools and conducting children's programs. They are also raising funds to take their hunger relief efforts to Brazil.

Whether it is constructing schools in Haiti, the Sudan, India, Guyana, and Ethiopia; or feeding the homeless in Huntsville, Philadelphia, Louisiana, and Mississippi, NAPS has consistently responded to disasters both next door and abroad and is willing, ready, and able to bring joy and relief to its neighbors. After years of service with NAPS and witnessing the miracles of changed lives, Brittany Law, a graduating senior at Oakwood College and an aspiring medical doctor, states, "I have devoted my life to rendering assistance to these people. My heart will always be with them. Their songs are forever on my lips." Every NAPS mission is special because when its volunteers leave, people know and understand, NAPS youth "don't just send relief, [they] hand-deliver it with love and care."

For more information about NAPS or to contribute to it, visit **www. napsoc.org**.

Following are testimonials from two more NAPS volunteers: Lenworth Anthony Sealey and Brittany Elise Wimberly.

Lenworth Anthony Sealey[3]

As a young man growing up in New York City, somehow along the way I developed a hard heart. As I walked among those who were willing to do just about anything to survive in a world where no one seemed to care, I learned to ignore the voices. Whether someone asked for directions or for a quarter, I wasn't interested in making myself vulnerable to some stranger who may have ill intentions concealed within his breast. I learned to close my eyes as well, shutting out the drugs, violence, and the homeless that dotted the streets of the city. However, when I joined NAPS, my eyes were peeled open and my ears unstopped forever.

I was privileged to go with this organization to Zambia, Africa, in the summer of 2004. Being able to see with my own eyes the struggles of the people of that region and to hear with my own ears their pleas

---

[3] Lenworth Anthony Sealey is a recent Oakwood College graduate. He has decided to dedicate another year to volunteering with NAPS. His rationale? "The God-given opportunity to serve mankind has brought me the most joy and has made the most significant impact on my life."

totally obliterated the "box" in which I had been enclosed for so many years. As I lived among them for that period, it helped me to realize that they are no different from me; they were all human beings. The experience also helped me to realize how fortunate I was and how selfish I had been with the resources that had been afforded me. As I returned home, my mindset was forever altered.

Bombarded by the messages of today's society, many people have become hard-hearted and self-centered. There is a prevailing belief among many individuals that the world somehow revolves around him or her. Therefore, what happens to others is inconsequential to him or her. This is a false concept that creates a perspective that makes it difficult to empathize with others, be it coworkers, classmates, neighbors, and sometimes family.

However, by making presentations at various institutions, including schools and juvenile detention centers, we seek to open the eyes and ears of people, especially the youth. As they see what's taking place in the world around them and as they hear the testimonies of youth making a positive impact on society, oftentimes the "box" in which one can become enclosed by focusing on one's self all the time just crumbles. These youth are then enabled to feel the pain of others and to feel the magnitude of the need in the world at large, becoming pressed upon to make it practical and personal. And finally, with softer, more sensitive hearts, they are empowered to go out and do likewise in their own personal sphere of influence. With every young person who commits himself or herself to serving others, the tide is steadily turned in favor of unity and love, thus affecting the world at large, for each little kindness sends its ripples throughout the ocean of humanity.

Brittany Elise Wimberly[4]

The most convenient utensil is a pencil because it allows you to erase mistakes. Is it possible to write without needing to erase a mis-

---

[4] Brittany Elise Wimberly is a sophomore biology education major at Oakwood College. She is dedicating the current school year to helping people in need nationally and internationally with NAPS. Although she is only 19 years old, "Nothing gives me greater joy than volunteering. If one desires to have a fulfilling sense of purpose, I encourage them to volunteer. It is truly a privilege and an honor to serve."

take? As a member of NAPS, I have witnessed God truly using ordinary young people to do extraordinary things.

I am privileged to be a member of this organization. NAPS has given me a purpose and a reason to share with others how I made it out of the depths of situations and circumstances. Whether one lives in the worst projects or in an elegant mansion, everyone is a victim of bad situations and circumstances.

On my first NAPS Saturday mission, I met this precious little girl named Danita who was nine years old and the second oldest of five children. Unfortunately, she did not live in a six-bedroom house at the top of the hill with a white picket fence, a spacious yard in the front and the back, and a dog. She did have loving and hardworking parents. For an entire year, I would pick her up on Saturday mornings, and we would walk to the NAPS children's program held at the center in her neighborhood. This program taught her Christian morals and, most importantly, let her know that she was special and there was no one else like her. My visiting Danita helped to prevent her from remaining in her current circumstances. I have faith that Danita will go to college, be successful, and mentor another precious little girl.

It seemed as if only Danita's life was changed, but she changed my whole outlook on life as well. She showed me through her unconditional love for me that I was special. She did not care that I could not quote the definition of a limit without studying it for hours. Neither did she mind that I did not know every answer to all her questions. It never bothered her that I made a B in biology. She did not disown me because I was not the best at everything. Danita gave me a reason to study countless hours, write a 30-page paper, and take mind-boggling exams. She turned my life story from a seeming sob story to a story that encourages me that God is able to pull anyone out of any situation. I was going to school for her and the countless other young ladies and little girls I have met while in NAPS. Regardless of the state or city, I always meet a little girl, a teenager, or a woman who has a similar background, has the same name or birthday, or is a carbon copy of myself.

"Children helping children" is one of NAPS's mottos. Everyone has a story about his or her life. A person's struggles, successes, failures, and setbacks are comprised in his or her personal story. A wise man once wrote: "There is nothing new under the sun." The same issues I have, as an African-American young woman in the year 2006, were the same issues a young colored woman in the late 1800s and early 1900s had. On the surface the struggle seems different, but its true identity is later revealed.

Survey all the people in your life. It's just about guaranteed that someone in your life is struggling with something you struggled with before. You have a responsibility to help that person, not only because it will make you feel extremely special, but that person will also be encouraged to help someone else. Ultimately, the whole world can be changed just by a simple gesture; it takes only one person to make a difference. Will you be that one person? Compassion negates the need for an eraser. Having compassion for that coworker, friend, neighbor, homeless person, or the stranger in the grocery store line can prevent most of the problems in this country. The person next to you is not just a person, but also your family. Your Danita! Danita's future now offers greater possibilities. Her could-have-been future of teen pregnancy, violence, alcoholism, and failure is as if it never was.

Hip-Hop Activism[5]

Dream with your eyes wide open . . .
— Toni Blackman

Hip-Hop is the greatest cultural phenomenon since the Harlem Renaissance. I've traveled to over 16 countries as a musical ambassador, performing, lecturing, and teaching. Whether in Senegal or Swaziland, in Taiwan or New York, there seems to be a universal thread that ties each of us together. Music and art have the power to heal, uplift, and touch the soul. I have been on the quest to harness that power to

---

[5] This essay is contributed by Toni Blackman, founder of the Freestyle Cipher Workshop. She is the first-ever Hip-Hop artist to travel with the U.S. Department of State as a cultural ambassador for Hip-Hop. Touring Senegal, Ghana, Southern Africa, and Southeast Asia as an American Cultural Specialist, she has performed in South Africa, the Netherlands, Germany, England, France, and Spain. She has shared the stage with Erykah Badu, Mos Def, The Roots, Wu Tang Clan, Me'Shell, Sarah McLachlan, Sheryl Crow, and Rickie Lee Jones. Her first book, Inner-Course (Villard/Random House), was published in 2003. The former Echoing Green Fellow recently completed a fellowship with the Soros Foundation's OSI. AOL BlackVoices named Blackman, who earned both her undergraduate and graduate degrees from Howard University, as one of the top ten African-American Next Generation Leaders to watch.

bring voice to the voiceless and to expand communication. Every day in classrooms around the world, artists like me retain a sense of idealism and have a glimmer of hope that we might be able to make a difference in the black community while making a living. Hip-Hop, born in the mid-1970s, now spans across three generations, and within my own I know several artists teaching everything—DJing, dance, visual art, spoken-word poetry, rap, and beat making. They teach in schools, after-school programs, shelters, and prisons. These artists are activists giving young people a medium to make their voices heard and to create change in their lives.

For me the commitment to combine rap with social change began on my first assignment with the U.S. Department of State, when I traveled to Dakar, Senegal. Towards the end of my stay, at a national press conference, journalists and reporters began to pepper me with all kinds of questions. After stumbling through questions related to economics, education, and identity, I began to feel defensive. They wanted to know what the African-American community intended to do to strengthen its relationship with Africa. They asked what were Hip-Hoppers' plans to address prison privatization, poverty, and crime. In my mind I thought, "I am a rapper, a poet; why are you asking me that?!" In the car on the way back to my hotel, the cultural attaché from the American Embassy—a brother from the states—reminded me that this is what the work is about; this is a part of our mission and our responsibility as cultural ambassadors.

Reflecting on this responsibility and after other thought-provoking and moving experiences, I was led in 1994 to found the Freestyle Union Cipher Workshop. Our mission is to not only use Hip-Hop as a form of artistic and cultural expression, but also to promote positive images and encourage activism within the rap community. From the beginning, rappers—ages 13 to 35, high-school dropouts and college educated, the UPS man, a biology teacher, and an art student—would sit in a cipher (circle) and freestyle (improvise) on a variety of topics, with one thing in common besides our love of Hip-Hop: we were all seeking a space where it was safe to be creative. I've facilitated thousands of Freestyle Union Ciphers all over the world and have never had an incident of violence. Over the years, I discovered that once a person is provided with the tools he/she needs to be creative and express himself or herself, to exercise the mind as a muscle, that the need for aggressive lyrics automatically decreases.

Freestyle Union has given me a forum to prepare Hip-Hop artists to function as educators and to engage them in social activism and community responsibility opportunities through events such as the "End the Silence" cipher, where each artist has to improvise on topics related to ending violence against women. Hip-Hop is not a band-aid, nor is it a quick fix for what ails education or the other issues in our community; however, it offers us access to various forms of creative outlets, which can ultimately lead us to having more balance in and control of our lives.

My most recent endeavor, "I Rhyme Like A Girl," a Freestyle Union initiative, is an intensive artist-development project for girls and women. As opposed to complaining about images and misogyny, my intention is to do something about it by developing a community of female voices that can not only hold their own, but also see themselves as leaders capable of impacting change. The representations of black female sexuality leave much to be desired, and the absence of female voices is representative of just how far we have *not* come. Ironically, it is in this latest endeavor that I've come to see Hip-Hop can be used as a tool for healing and spiritual wellness. Many of the women are building self-confidence and self-esteem, developing leadership and communication skills, while addressing childhood issues such as sexual abuse, rape, and abandonment. It is said that one can measure how civilized a society is by how it treats its women and children. Honoring the voices of our young sisters is an important next step in healing our relationships with one another.

In the same way that we would never allow pop radio or television to define jazz for us, as we would not trust the mainstream media to educate us on the history of slavery or the Middle Passage, we must not accept the story that is being told about our youth and Hip-Hop because it is only being half-told. Hip-Hop is a rich culture permeated by the presence of Africanisms that have survived for centuries. When we go beneath the surface, we not only find creativity and tradition, but we can also find a medium for social change and maybe—most importantly—hope.

Succeeding Against All Odds . . .[6]

The greatest menace to freedom is an inert people.

— Louis Brandeis
U.S. Supreme Court Justice, 1916–1939

When I became a lawyer, one of my first jobs was as a public defender charged with representing teenaged clients accused of committing serious crimes in Washington, DC. In case after case, I watched our government invest astonishing resources into locking children away. There was money for police, money for prosecutors, money for expert witnesses, and ultimately money for years and years of prison. It was not long before I became well versed in the sobering statistics: while it cost only about eight-thousand dollars a year to educate a child, it cost about 40-thousand dollars to lock him up. And yet, society's willingness to invest seemed boundless.

As I tried to digest the dynamics of this situation, I began to ask myself questions. Why are we all here *now*? Why do we feign concern for these children *now*? When these children were being abused at home and ignored at school, where were we *then*? Though my clients had committed acts that were wrong, society's collective failure to intervene earlier in their lives was also wrong.

I am the son of a civil rights legend. Adhering to a principle of *inaction* is not exactly my strongpoint. In my view, I had no alternative other than to act and no better place to start than the schools. As I prepared for action, I reflected on the education system I witnessed firsthand with many of my clients. I saw auto repair classes with no cars, shop classes with no wood, and other "alternative education" classes where equipment and instruction were lacking. I witnessed

---

[6] This essay is authored by James Forman, Jr., son of the legendary civil rights activist, James Forman, Sr. A graduate of Brown University and Yale Law School, Forman is an Associate Professor of Law at Georgetown University Law Center, where he teaches and writes in the areas of criminal procedure and education law. Following graduation from Yale, he served as a judicial clerk for U.S. Supreme Court Justice Sandra Day O'Connor. His interest in educational programs for at-risk and court-involved youth led him to start, along with a colleague, the Maya Angelou Public Charter School in Washington, DC, in 1997. The school is recognized as one of the most successful programs of its kind in the country, combining rigorous education, job training, counseling, mental health services, life skills, and dormitory living for school dropouts and youth who have previously been incarcerated. The school currently has two campuses in the District, with a third one set to come onboard in late 2007.

teachers who used videos to control high school classes because it was easier than actually teaching. History teaches us about the importance of education to advancement in our society. But still, more than 50 years after *Brown v. Board of Education,* we have an education system that in too many cities is immoral and too often merely feeds our equally immoral and ineffective criminal justice system.

And so, I decided to act. I started by talking to my clients about the kind of program that would have made a difference in their lives. My good friend David Domenici and I started a school to serve children such as my clients. We worked zealously and grew quickly beholden to our dream. We were secure with confidence that if we had love, high expectations, and an unyielding belief in the greatness of each young man and woman, our students would achieve success.

While our optimism then seemed slightly implausible, today it has proved itself to be both authentic and contagious. We have grown into a space called the Maya Angelou Public Charter School, and our school *and* our students are thriving. We have two campuses and serve 250 students. Our doors are open from 9:30 a.m. to 7:15 p.m., with mandatory after-school electives, dinner, and an hour of one-on-one tutoring nightly. Historically, almost one-third of our students had some contact with the juvenile justice system. Many had essentially dropped out of school; at least half of them qualify as special education students. Yet 70 percent of our graduates go on to college. The numbers speak for themselves.

Over 250 people volunteer at our school each week. We have comprehensive mental health services on site with a psychologist and three social workers; we have 15 students who live in our residential homes; our students have internships where they learn job skills and earn money; and we run a mandatory six-week summer program for all students. We do this because our students need it and deserve it.

When you are fed up, you either shut down or act. The options are that straightforward. Doing nothing renders you inert and is detrimental to freedom and democracy. As a lawyer, an educator, and, most importantly, an activist, I have rejected the path of inertness in favor of intentional action to help society collectively intervene in the lives of children.

For more information about the Maya Angelou Public Charter School, visit **www.seeforever.org**.

Education Plus Action Equals Change[7]

The black family's median net worth is $8,300, or *seven times* less than the white family's median net worth of $56,000, according to editors Melvin Oliver and Thomas Shapiro in their groundbreaking book, *Black Wealth, White Wealth* (Routledge, 2006). Earl Graves, Jr., of *Black Enterprise* magazine, adds, "Blacks on the average are six times more likely than whites to buy a Mercedes, and the average income of an African American who buys a Jaguar is about one-third less than that of a white purchaser of the luxury vehicle." These are staggering statistics and have been the driving force behind my current profession.

It really began for me in 2002, when I attended a financial empowerment seminar and was moved by the number of people discussing this issue. There wasn't enough time to field the multitude of questions being fired towards the presenters. However, the next day, just before stores were opening, I walked past a shoe store and noticed a long line in front. I recognized one of the participants from the previous day's financial empowerment seminar standing in line with her son. It was easy to remember her because she had asked many of the questions at the seminar and, in doing so, painted a very grim personal financial picture of her own circumstances. After re-introducing ourselves, I asked the purpose of the line, and she shamefully responded, "They are releasing the new Jordans and I wanted to purchase them for my seven-year-old child." I walked away knowing that the black community was in need of more than simply education; knowledge by itself is not power. Knowledge plus action equals power, and it was time to take action.

I am now President of Optimum Capital Management, a company I launched to address the economic problems within the black community. It was established because the financial planning industry has

---

[7] This essay is contributed by Ryan C. Mack, President of Optimum Capital Management, LLC. After graduating from the nation's top business school—the University of Michigan, he gained employment in various positions within the high-finance arena. Ultimately, Mack discovered his life mission: to build and to develop a durable financial empire geared towards educating clients within his community and beyond. He charitably lends his support to inner-city communities by coordinating workshops teaching the basic principles of understanding the power of financial planning. Unions, churches, government-subsidized housing communities, PAL programs, nonprofits, and especially colleges and universities have benefited from the financial literacy classes/workshops that he has developed and instructed.

long neglected the need for financial education in the community. As a company, we instill principles of accountability and responsibility within a community plagued by high consumption and debt levels. Optimum Capital Management is committed to providing highly skilled, full-service financial planning in the most cost-efficient means for our clients. While we are a for-profit company with a significant clientele, we are committed to the needs of the community.

I didn't always know that I would take this route. In 1999 I graduated from the University of Michigan Business School with a concentration in finance. During the next five years as a trader on Wall Street, I began to develop an interest in the significance of financial literacy within the African-American community. I established my own financial awareness group in 2003 and began to write biweekly newsletters, informing subscribers of important principles of financial literacy for people of all income levels.

Wanting to pursue a full-time career in financial planning, in 2004 I decided to interview for positions with financial planning firms, only to discover the expectation that as an employee of these firms, I was to service solely high-net-worth individuals. This expectation was not in alignment with my own values and commitment to the community.

Armed with words of wisdom from my grandmother before I moved to New York from Detroit ("Don't lose yourself when you go out there, boy.") and with an enhanced spiritual connection with God, I was directed to create my own company.

For the next 12 months I applied what I had been learning to create my own company by:

- Creating a business plan;
- Analyzing the company material of those firms who had previously offered me employment;
- Networking with other entrepreneurs to discuss business strategies; and
- Acquiring membership with Crown Financial Ministries and serving as volunteer Budget Coach using biblical principles to assist others with their financial planning strategies.

During my last three years on Wall Street, before I started the company, I volunteered weekly, working with inner-city youth in the community. I established an organization, Leaders of Tomorrow (LOT), for students grades three through eight who were taught the values of leadership, unity, and commitment through stepping (a fraternity pastime). Upon establishing my own company, the knowledge of the value of LOT resulted in my decision to establish another youth organization more aligned with the principles of my company.

In 2004, I launched All About Business (AAB), designed to increase financial awareness of high school students. One day a week during the school year, Benjamin Banneker Academy students in Brooklyn, New York, studied principles of financial literacy, current events, business etiquette, networking, and entrepreneurship. They were successful in learning about financial literacy, and the program opened up many opportunities for them: One received a Bill Gates scholarship fully funded through his earning his Ph.D. degree. Two received offers from INROADS, which trains and develops talented minority students for professional careers in business and industry. Another received a $5,000 scholarship; all have a portfolio of published financial literacy newsletters to submit to their next potential employer.

During the first few months of Optimum Capital Management, several other educational programs were launched, including: free workshops in inner-city housing developments throughout the East Coast; financial workshops geared to train union employees to navigate through the obstacles of an unstable economy; publishing newsletters and numerous articles; and financial empowerment programs to institute within schools for the benefit of teachers, parents, and students.

Optimum Capital Management recognizes how tremendous the tasks are that must be accomplished. Many factors account for the economic and social status of African Americans, some of which are not directly within our control. However, there is a lot that *is* within our control. "The black dollar turns over less than once on average before it leaves the community," reports Lee Jenkins in *Taking Care of Business: Establishing a Financial Legacy for Your Family* (Lift Every Voice, 2001). "Asians turn over their money nine times in their communities, and whites turn their money over eight times before it leaves." Without the basic knowledge of how to control our finances, without being equipped or supplied with an ability to think for ourselves, we are not empowered and are at the mercy of others.

I have made a life commitment to God that I will do all that is necessary to assure that my community is not only educated of these empowering principles, but that they can also use Optimum as a means to implement the proper solutions within their lives. A paradigm shift is needed to start this movement in our communities; our actions thus far have not been successful. Optimum will create the change that is necessary in our communities and beyond. This is my commitment, and I will continue to do God's work by any means necessary.

THE COVENANT *In Action:*
The Toolkit for Next Steps

Moving from the promise of the *Covenant with Black America* to sustained community action begins with everyday people getting together, sharing views about what changes they want to see in their community, and working together over time to develop and carry out a plan for social change.

The two-part toolkit that follows begins by looking at how well-known organizing and advocacy approaches can be used to advance *The Covenant* goals. Then, we introduce some new, lesser-known but equally powerful strategies for action. The purpose of all these strategies is to get people in communities together and to help you engage with each other so that you can define your own challenges, discover ways of overcoming them, and identify the resources you need to meet your objectives.

Part I of this toolkit, prepared by PolicyLink, presents a step-by-step guide to advocacy that will help you build your arguments for change, bring others into your action campaigns, select and develop effective strategies, and build broad public support to advance your cause. Sometimes the only recourse to fight an injustice is to hire a lawyer, while there are other times when bringing an injustice to the attention of an elected official is sufficient. To help you maneuver through all these and other questions and steps, Part I is organized into categories that focus on: how to get the facts and information about a problem; how to organize and build coalitions; how to develop targeted goals and strategies; and how to communicate to build support and momentum, including how to harness the power of the Internet.

Part II, produced by The Jamestown Project, reflects upon the conventional advocacy tools presented in Part I and offers novel approaches to communicating. These innovative communication tools emphasize the importance of dialogue and shared values in building engagement and commitment that is sustained over time by being grounded in a deep understanding of the experiences and aspirations of others. This section highlights the power of the following tools and strategies: storytelling/story sharing; Reflective Community Practice; The World Café model; Citizen Deliberative Councils, and Study Circles. All of these strategies can be combined in multiple ways and used in conjunction with the conventional advocacy strategies presented in Part I to connect people, deeply enabling them to engage in *sustained, coordinated, long-term* action to achieve real and effective change. Combining these strategies can help bridge gaps among generations; promote community learning; create new knowledge; strengthen relationships; move an advocacy agenda; and foster inclusion, participation, and other core democratic values.

PART I: ADVOCATING FOR CHANGE

Achieving the goals of the *Covenant with Black America* must involve advocacy. Advocacy can happen in many different ways. It can involve seeking changes in government agency policies or practices, working with private businesses, changing laws, introducing ballot initiatives, creating public pressure, and, when necessary, litigating. Choosing the best advocacy strategy will depend on the specific problem, the solutions sought, the resources available, the receptivity of decision makers, and other factors.

This toolkit describes the basic advocacy strategies, their advantages and disadvantages, what to consider in choosing among them, and the basic steps for an advocacy campaign. In addition to the information provided in each section, this toolkit includes extensive references; for more detail about specific strategies and examples of the positive outcomes that effective advocacy efforts can deliver, consult the PolicyLink online resource, *Advocating for Change,* at **www.policy link.org**. Another valuable resource tool, also found at this website, is *Organized for Change: The Activist's Guide to Police Reform,* which uses advocacy tools and strategies to advance community-centered policing and police reform efforts.

Bringing about needed meaningful changes is hard work and takes time, but the rewards are great. Advocacy can lead to the results you seek and can move you closer to ensuring that people of all races and income levels participate and prosper.

What Is an Advocate?

An advocate is someone who speaks for or pleads the case for oneself or for another. While lawyers do this for a living, far more often parents, teachers, neighbors, workers, and church, civic, nonprofit, and community leaders are called on to advocate for the changes needed to achieve greater equity in their communities. They advocate on issues that matter to them, such as employment, education, housing, healthcare, and transportation. Most people have the basic skills to be an advocate—knowing what is important, working with others, planning, and ably communicating what needs to be done.

This toolkit shows how to use these skills to make a compelling case before decision makers and persuade them to take corrective action. Advocacy is most effective when a broad range of people lend their individual skills, time, and support to a campaign focused on making change happen.

Effective advocacy is based on four elements:

- Getting the facts;
- Organizing support;
- Making a plan; and
- Communicating a clear and compelling story
  of what is wrong and what should be done.

Key Information

Restrictions on Legislative Advocacy

Nonprofit charitable organizations (those covered under Internal Revenue Code 501(c) (3)) can lobby. In fact, Congress has passed legislation that gives these charitable organizations the right to lobby (within designated limits) and has stated that influencing legislation is an appropriate and a legitimate activity.

There are many ways to lobby or advocate in legislatures without violating Internal Revenue Service (IRS) rules. Under IRS definitions, there are two types of legislative advocacy or lobbying—*direct* and *grassroots*—and there are annual limits on the amount that can be spent on each by charitable organizations. Direct lobbying includes three elements: expressing a point of view on a specific piece of legislation; direct communication to a legislator, her or his staff, or another involved government employee; and requesting an action (such as to support, oppose, or amend a bill). Grassroots lobbying is defined as expressing a point of view on a piece of legislation and seeking to influence others (the public) to take specific action, such as writing to a legislator to oppose a specific bill.

These restrictions do not apply to many other (nonlobbying) forms of advocacy, such as organizing and building community support, creating public pressure, or talking to the staff of a government agency about regulatory changes.

Electioneering—supporting or opposing a candidate for public office—is strictly prohibited and carries serious potential penalties, including an organization's losing its charitable nonprofit status.

To find out more about what is permitted, limited, and prohibited and what rules might apply to your organization, see *Worry-Free Lobbying for Nonprofits* and other materials published by The Alliance for Justice (**www.allianceforjustice.org/**). These materials clearly describe the guidelines for

501(c)(3) organizations to follow when advocating before city councils, county boards of supervisors, state legislatures, the Congress, or on ballot measures.

In addition, some states and local governments may require you to register as a lobbyist.

Check the website or contact the office of the city or county clerk, or the secretary of state, for more information.

Getting the Facts

The first step is to get the facts. Finding out what is wrong, who is hurt, and the extent and cause of the problem is critical to effective advocacy. Solid facts, data, and strong analysis will help you define the problem, identify solutions, enlist others to support your efforts, overcome opposition, communicate to reporters, and convince decision makers.

You can get the facts in several ways. On any given issue, there is already a lot of information in newspaper articles, published reports, scientific studies, and government documents. Much of this is quickly and easily accessible, readable, and understandable. It can also be useful to gather information firsthand; for example, by interviewing people in your community to see who is being hurt by a problem and how.

You can get the facts by getting answers to the following types of questions:

- Who is being hurt and what needs to be corrected?
- How are they being hurt? How can you describe the problem? For example, is the problem a lack of transportation to jobs, a shortage of affordable housing, high unemployment, pollution, or obstacles to economic development?
- How serious and widespread is the problem?
- If left unaddressed, will the problem get more or less serious?
- If more serious, how?
- How is the community affected?

To design an effective campaign strategy, you should know the following.

About the problem:

- If it is long-standing, why hasn't it been resolved?
- What agencies, businesses, corporations, or organizations are causing or responsible for addressing it?
- Are there any laws or rules related to it?
- What reasons are given to justify it?
- Who knows about it?
- Who thinks that there is a problem?
- Who thinks that there isn't?

About possible solutions:

- What are they?
- How much will they cost? What will be the benefits? Are there ancillary benefits?
- What are the politics of the situation (i.e., who has the power to correct the problem and what constituencies, facts, arguments, etc., are likely to persuade her or him to take action)?
- Have any actions been taken? If so, with what results?
- What reports or news accounts have there been?
- What has happened in other areas? Have workable solutions been found?

Government agencies are often a source of valuable information. Local and national agencies collect data, conduct or fund research studies, and publish policy papers and reports. Also check with local colleges and universities. Many professors and graduate students are interested in working on problems that are immediately relevant to the wider community. When combined with the information you have gathered at the community level, this kind of research can be extremely powerful in documenting the seriousness of the problem you are concerned about and the effectiveness of the solutions you propose.

If necessary, put together a small team of people and divide the work. Use the preceding list as a checklist, modifying it to fit your problem. Chances are that you won't find all of the answers at once. Keep asking questions. Meet regularly to share what you have learned, mark your progress, and plan the next steps.

At this stage, you are trying to find out as much as you can about the problem. Be thorough and keep an open mind. Later you will ask community members, potential supporters, reporters, decision makers, and the public at large to rely on what you say. Your credibility will be on the line and, with it, your ability to be effective.

Where to Find the Information

Books, newspapers, and periodicals. Read the literature on the problem and its history, not only to know everything you can, but also to identify those who may be helpful as well as those who may be part of the problem.

The Internet. A search may uncover information about your problem and links to relevant organizations in other places.

Government reports and documents. Your efforts will gain credibility if they are supported by information from government sources. Building a credible campaign means building the case to make it difficult to deny that a problem exists.

Community members. Conversations with people—young and old and of different races and ethnicities—who are harmed by the problem are critical to understanding the nature and extent of the problem. They can bring real-life experiences into the discussion and offer meaningful solutions. Keep an eye out for stories you may want to highlight later and for potential spokespersons for news conferences, interviews with reporters, hearings, and meetings with decision makers.

Organizations and individuals. It is extremely important to learn the views of other organizations and individuals interested in the problem you are concerned about. You'll want to confer with like-minded individuals and organizations, both to get the benefit of their experience and to enlist their support. The best information about community conditions and resources often comes from local nonprofit organizations and research groups. You should also find out the positions of potential opponents both to better understand their perspectives and to help you incorporate effective arguments against their positions in your campaign.

Experts. One way to identify the experts on your issue is to take note of the names mentioned or quoted in news articles, studies, reports, etc. Another is to ask a state or national organization whom it would go to for information on this kind of problem.

Putting together accurate information with accessible language will help you make your case and achieve the desired results.

Organizing Support: Building Effective Coalitions. A single individual or an organization can call for action alone, but the likelihood of success is far greater if a coalition of groups and individuals join in the effort.

Organizing builds power. Uniting large numbers of people around a specific issue or campaign enables you to wield the kind of influence that other people have because they make large campaign contributions or have powerful positions in business, society, or government. Organizing alerts decision makers to the potential political consequences of their actions. It reminds elected and appointed officials that you can affect how long they stay in office or whether they advance to a higher one. The media are more likely to take notice when you can draw a crowd that shows strong support for your cause.

Organizing gives you staying power. To achieve and maintain reform requires sustained effort. Few organizations have the staff and resources to accomplish this alone. Organizing identifies and develops the leaders, staff skills, and resources you need to sustain progress over time.

Organizing can produce real improvement in people's lives in addition to tangible changes that joint efforts achieve. Organizing also builds community through collective problem-solving and instills in people a personal sense of power to effect change.

Organizing is bringing people together to develop a collective vision for their community, to achieve a common goal, and to fight a battle that is more likely to be won if many stand up together instead of just a few. Organizing is working with others in the community to learn what is wrong, what needs to be done, and how to work together. It is recruiting others to join and keeping people motivated to stay with it over the long haul.

Coalition building takes the concept of organizing from individuals to organizations. It brings organizations together to focus on an issue or a problem. Sometimes coalition members share a specific goal, such as getting the city to establish a fund to expand recreation activities for young people. Other times they may join because of principles, such as the need for affordable housing in general or a desire to end homelessness.

Coalitions allow for pooling of resources, skills, experience, contacts, strategies, and ideas for solutions. A broad-based coalition can add tremendous power to your effort: decision makers notice when organizations representing multiple constituencies they care about unify around a list of shared concerns or demands. Coalitions give decision makers added incentive to agree to proposed solutions because the leaders can thereby satisfy the demands of several constituencies at once. Coalitions are critical to attacking problems that affect more than one community.

Successful Coalition Components

Begin building your coalition by reaching out to individuals and organizations that are recognized and respected, both by your community and the wider public. Having a prominent person as a leader and strong organizations as members can make it easier for others to join you. Meet with them to discuss the problem, seek their ideas and opinions, and ask for their support. Try to include organizations that are considered to be knowledgeable. Agencies and the media will treat you more seriously if the coalition includes organizations with a history of action and experience. (Sometimes these organizations don't exist. Sometimes your problem may be so new or localized that you are the first one to attack it. If so, reach out to organizations in neighboring communities or with related interests, inform them about the problem you are concerned with, and, if they seem supportive, invite them to join your coalition.)

Many groups may be willing to be part of an effort if you recognize that different organizations can help in different ways. Seek to understand each organization's specific interests and needs. Because of limited resources and ongoing work on other issues, organizations will vary the depth of their involvement in different efforts. Choose strategies that build from as many organizations' strengths and priorities as possible. Be prepared to facilitate and coordinate a process to build understanding and trust across different organizations and community leaders. This will take time, but a broad coalition will bring greater strength than one that includes organizations focused only on a specific issue. As you build your coalition, reach out to include politically diverse groups. The broader the ethnic, racial, economic, political, and geographic representation is, the more powerful the coalition. It is much harder to dismiss an effort supported by a wide range of organizations, especially if those organizations are often not on the same side.

CASE STUDY: Building a Regional Coalition Across Issues and Constituencies

The unprecedented economic boom of the 1990s revitalized the Greater Boston economy, re-establishing one of the nation's preferred metropolitan regions. Simultaneously, existing inequities deepened as the gulf between high-skill, high-wage jobs and low-skill, low-wage service positions widened. This gulf exacerbated race and income disparities. Affordable housing remained disconnected from economic opportunities spread throughout the region as Massachusetts became the least affordable housing market in the nation.

Advocacy efforts led to public forums that brought together 165 diverse representatives from nonprofits and government to explore opportunities that realign public policies to advance equitable development. As a result, some of the area's leading advocacy organizations—working to achieve affordable housing, economic development, environmental justice, transportation equity, and community development—created a new coalition, Action for Regional Equity (Action!).

Forming a regional coalition focused on equitable development across multiple jurisdictions and different issues has not been without challenges. Initial steps involved building trust and relationships and highlighting the connections across interests, issues, and constituencies. Developing the coalition's agenda required constant attention to balancing each organization's priorities and finding common ground in each year's policy objective.

In 2004, Action! advocated for equity principles in adopting new incentives for housing near public transportation. Action! questioned the equity of proposed fare hikes, pushed for balanced transit-oriented development, and called for new housing revenue sources, serving families at levels affordable to their income. Collective planning strengthened the coalition.

Action! has provided public comment on critical state policy, lobbied for legislative changes that advance regional equity, provided significant support to the campaign efforts of allies, and led its own policy campaign during 2006 focused on data collection for the commonwealth's affordable housing investment. In 2006–2007, Action! is focusing on critical issues in affordable housing and transportation equity, commencing with findings from its recently released reports on the opportunities to increase housing in nonprofit and community control, and ways to ensure equity in the growth of transit-oriented development throughout the commonwealth.

New leadership is emerging, new alliances are being developed, and old ones strengthened. A multi-issue, regional coalition is making significant progress toward equitable development.

Coalitions are strongest when:

- All coalition members agree on the fundamental goal and the plan to achieve it.
- There is leadership with the time, skills, experience, resources, and coalition support to do the job.
- There is a clear understanding about each coalition member's level of participation. For example, some organizations may want to sign on from the

beginning; others may be more comfortable sending letters of support; some may be able to do some limited surveys in their community; some may be able to have a representative testify if there is a public hearing; others may want to play a leadership role and participate fully. Those representing business may want to play only an insider role. Make it possible for members to contribute to the effort in many different ways, according to their resources and priorities.

- There is a commitment to full, thorough communication.

- Members understand how decisions will be made. There will likely be instances when decisions need to be made quickly. Will the leadership of the coalition (a person, one organization, or a small executive committee of members) have the authority to make the decision? If so, what kinds of decisions can it make? Should coalition members be polled before some decisions are made? If so, which decisions, and how should members be polled (e-mail, fax, phone)? How quickly will coalition members need to respond?

- Coalition members present a united front and choose speakers or representatives, giving them the necessary decision-making authority.

- Members agree on the style of the campaign. Will it be hard and aggressive or soft and diplomatic? Will the campaign aim for high visibility or work behind the scenes?

- Work is divided according to each member's strengths, resources, capacity, and experience in organizing, research, use of the media, negotiating skills, and leadership.

- Credit is shared, and each member is recognized for her or his contribution.

- All members are in it for the long term and support each other's interests, until the job is done, with no selling out or side deals.

- Successes are celebrated.

A strong coalition makes the work easier and more likely to succeed. Begin building your coalition early. Share your information with supporters. Ask them what they think about your proposed solution. Invite their ideas. Define the problem and solution jointly instead of going it alone.

Coalitions can be formal, having their own letterhead, staff, and separate office, or as informal as simply an agreement to support a single goal. If possible, you want supporters to sign on as sponsors of an effort or a campaign, but, if an organization cannot join fully in the work, welcome a letter of support or testimony at a public hearing. Always be conscious that each organization's priorities and capabilities will differ; not every group will participate in the front line of the campaign.

Tensions

Coalition building is difficult. Coalitions must support a shared vision of what to do and how to do it. Based on your fact-finding and analysis, you may have reached conclusions about what is wrong and what needs to be done. However, before you become wedded to your conclusions and goals and launch your effort, present your supporters with the information you have gathered and see what they think the problems and solutions are. Advocacy is a joint effort, and your partners need to help make key decisions and take ownership of the campaign. If there is no agreement on the problem or solution, or if community members or organizations can't agree on roles, leadership, or strategy, the work will be much more difficult and less likely to succeed. Reaching an agreement on these issues may require patience, compromise, and time. Different styles and approaches may have to be bridged.

If you are trying to build a multiracial, multicultural coalition, you may find that racial issues may have to be explored and addressed, and cultural differences may have to be understood and appreciated. Keeping a coalition together is ongoing; even when there is initial agreement about the problem and goals, members may have different views about strategic decisions, the specific language for a news release, or the message or tone for the campaign. Some may express their opinions strongly and seem unwilling to consider the views of others. Some partners may be raring to get started, while others may be unable to participate because of short-term deadlines they need to meet on other issues. Working through these differences will take time but will make your campaign stronger in the end.

Key Information

Conducting a Power Analysis

Before setting out to organize your community or build a coalition, it's important to know which people and organizations have power and influence. Many individuals and institutions have influence, whether in the community, the government, or the private sector. Analyze who holds power, both formal and informal. Examine your own power, both what you already have and what you need. Analyzing the formal power structure will tell you who is officially in charge; analyzing the informal power structure will tell you the underlying reality of how decisions are really made and how things actually get done. Including people and organizations with either formal or informal power in your coalition will increase your power and the likelihood of success.

For more information on conducting a power analysis, consult *Advocating for Change*, at **www.policylink.org**, and "Power Analysis" in *Dynamics of Organizing*, available at **www.tenant.net/Organize/orgdyn.html**; "Conduct a power analysis" in *How—and Why—to Influence Public Policy: An Action Guide for Community Organizations*, **www.communitychange.org/publications/pubpolicy.htm**; and *Power and Organizing*, available at **www.grassrootspolicy.org/publications/power.html**.

Red Flags

When the opposition to your efforts is strong or perhaps hostile, you need to maintain internal accord. Allies, partners, coworkers, or supporters who become unhappy and break away from the agreed-on plan may undercut your work. Warning signals should go up:

- If coalition communications are not up to date;
- If information is not fully shared and available; and
- If differences of opinion among coalition members are set aside unresolved.

Remember: This is a campaign. You are trying to persuade decision makers, the media, and the public about the seriousness of a problem and the need for solutions to be adopted. This is building your community. In addition to solving a specific problem, advocacy campaigns build the community's capacity to work together to achieve important goals and to develop the leadership skills of those involved. A strong coalition of groups and individuals makes the work easier, more exciting, and more likely to succeed.

Making Your Plan: Developing Goals and Strategy

Every advocacy campaign requires a plan to get from the problem to the solution and a road map of the steps to be taken along the way. The plan should include:

- A clearly defined problem;
- A clearly defined solution and interim goals;
- An assessment of resources; and
- A clear strategy.

Define the Problem

Defining the problem may sound easy. In fact, there may be important differences in the way people in the same community view the issue. For example, some people may think that the community crime problem exists because of too few police officers serving the city, while others might believe that the problem is poor understanding between police and community. A common view about the problem will be important when reaching agreement about solutions. Take the above example: solving the problem of too few police officers might be a bond measure to increase the police force; but if the problem is poor police/community relations, a community policing program could be the best approach. Indeed, some may not perceive that the crime problem has anything to do with police, but is rather a result of too many unsupervised youth; this could lead to a solution that involves more after-school programs. Of course, problems are often multifaceted. Try to identify these differences early and work toward a consensus.

Working through these differences will test whether you are on the right track. Taking the time to define the problem will also help bring people together and convince others about exactly what needs to be fixed.

Define the Solution and Interim Goals

Next, define the solution to the problem. If the problem is complicated, set specific interim and long-term goals that will bring you closer to achieving the solution. Examples of short-term goals might be to educate and organize community members; form a coalition of community groups; reach out to organizations in neighboring communities and to regional and statewide groups; conduct surveys of residents and businesses in the community to document their support for specific solutions; and identify and educate reporters about the issue. Meeting measurable goals will allow the coalition to see that it is moving toward the ultimate solution and to demonstrate to the community that your campaign is serious about addressing the identified problem.

Regularly review your goals and assess your progress. Make changes to the plan if necessary.

Assess Your Resources

Assess the resources of the community and coalition members, particularly the ability to work together. Is there a history of working together? Can there be agreement on leadership? Are there enough people with the skills and experience to succeed? In addition to leadership, you need people with the skills to do surveys and gather facts and information to document any problems. Demonstrating support for your proposal will be important. Someone will need to get people out for meetings and for news conferences and other community events. You will need speakers who can represent the community or coalition. Is there a way to pay for supplies and reimburse out-of-pocket expenses, places to meet, and computers? Are there phones to call the mediator or the community to announce meetings? Is there someone who can manage e-mails and a website? If necessary, you may have to ask those who have these capabilities to join the campaign.

Local churches, community organizations, and individuals can often help. People's time for fact-gathering and community surveys, organizing, writing notices of meetings, and fulfilling other needs must be realistically assessed. The actual out-of-pocket dollar costs for an advocacy campaign may be minimal, from nothing to a few hundred dollars for telephones and copying. It is people's time that is needed most. But sometimes funds are needed—to support activities, bring in needed expertise, or provide staff support.

It is possible to find funds for advocacy campaigns. Individual donors may be willing to contribute to an effort to solve an important community problem. Special public fundraising efforts can be initiated. Foundations interested in social change, public policy, or specific issues can be consulted about funding elements of an advocacy campaign or ongoing advocacy work. Often coalition members, such as labor organizations, might contribute needed funds or services for a campaign.

A Clear Strategy

Now that you have decided what the problem is and its appropriate solution, the next step is to decide where you want to focus your efforts. Should you concentrate on local officials or state government, the state legislature, city council, or a government agency, the courts, private businesses, or some other institution? The basic ways to bring about change are:

- Working with private companies;
- Working with government agencies;
- Going to court;
- Changing the law;
- Using the initiative or referendum process;
- Creating your own forum; and
- Choosing the right advocacy strategy.

CASE STUDY: Advocating for Living Wages, Local Hiring, and Affordable Housing

In Los Angeles, the Figueroa Corridor Coalition for Economic Justice reached an historic agreement with the developers of a four-million-square-foot Sports and Entertainment District to be built adjacent to the Staples Center, a large existing sports arena. When the original Staples Center was developed, it encountered diffuse and fragmented complaints from the community that resulted in minimal concessions. However, two years later, when an expansion was proposed, the community was prepared. Community members had organized and educated themselves about the proposed expansion, developed a shared platform, and through unity came strength. Twenty-nine community groups, including local churches, environmental justice groups, and tenant-rights organizations, five labor unions, and 300 predominantly immigrant residents came together to advocate for living wages, jobs, affordable housing, and neighborhood parks. They argued that the developers, who were to receive at least $75 million in subsidies from the city, must be accountable to surrounding communities and to deliver benefits to residents.

After nearly 100 hours of negotiations, the Figueroa Coalition and developers agreed to the following:

- Living-Wage Jobs: Seventy percent of the 5,500 permanent jobs at the development will be union or pay at least a living wage, one that covers basic needs such as housing, food, transportation, and healthcare.
- Local Hiring: Local residents will be notified of jobs through a first-source hiring program set up by the coalition with $100,000 in seed money.
- Affordable Housing: Twenty percent of the housing units in the development will be affordable. An interest-free revolving predevelopment loan fund of $650,000 will help local nonprofits develop from 130 to 325 additional affordable units.
- Parks and Recreation: More than $1 million will be dedicated for the creation or improvement of parks within a mile of the project. The design process must include community input.

For community residents, higher wages, employment, affordable housing, and better parks were the result of organizing, coalition building, and effective advocacy.

Working with Private Companies

Private businesses have an enormous stake in improving education, transportation, housing, and the environment. Convincing private businesses to change their policies may require meeting with executives or department heads to solve a specific problem. It may also be necessary to urge businesses to be part of a larger alliance to reform the system itself through new laws, rules, structural changes, or incentives.

Considerations: Negotiating with a business will almost always result in less than what the community thinks is needed to solve a specific problem. Even if a solution proposed by a company is not ideal, it may improve the situation. Are you settling for too little or is it more than you can get through other strategies? Does accepting the company's offer foreclose you from pursuing other strategies? If so, for how long?

Pluses

- Since its public image is a valuable asset, a business may be especially willing to help address a specific problem if it enhances that image with consumers, shareholders, employees, government officials, and the media.
- Large corporations have resources that can be enormously helpful in bringing about change—money, of course, and also media and public relations resources, lobbying and governmental affairs staffs, and high-level contacts with other large businesses, foundations, and government.
- Getting one corporation to change may set standards for others to meet.
- Change by a large corporation can have an effect on its many suppliers.

Minuses

- Every business seeks profits. Typically, businesses will oppose proposals that might harm their economic interests, support those that further them, and be indifferent to ones that don't affect those interests.
- Businesses want public credit for working with community groups, sometimes even when they do little or nothing to address community concerns.
- Simply meeting with community groups, for instance, can be inflated by a corporate public relations department into "working closely with [your organization] to attack [your problem] in [your neighborhood.]"
- Many businesses have little or no experience working with community groups. They may therefore be hostile, suspicious, or slow to understand how their interests overlap with those of the community.

For more information about working with private companies, consult the Corporate Accountability Project, Researching Corporations at **www.corporations.org/research.html**; the Data Center, Impact Research for Social Justice at **www.datacenter.org**; and Environmental Defense, Alliance for Environmental Innovation at **www.environ mentaldefense.org./alliance**.

Working with Government Agencies

In the federal, state, and local governments, administrative agencies (departments, commissions, boards, etc.) are responsible for specific areas (education, housing, transportation, environment, planning and land use, health, etc.). Established by Congress, state legislatures, or city councils, administrative agencies are usually given broad powers to oversee business practices and to address problems in specified issue areas.

For example, many state agencies have the power to adopt, amend, or repeal rules and regulations that carry the same power as laws adopted by legislatures or city councils. They can also bring enforcement actions to stop practices that violate the law or agency rules and can fine and revoke the licenses of violators. Agencies also have the power to investigate problems and advise the executive branch (president, governor, or mayor) and the legislature on the need for new laws, programs, and other governmental actions to improve their effectiveness. There are several ways to try to influence how an agency serves your community. You may want to ask an elected representative to write or call an agency director and schedule a meeting, inviting community coalition leaders to join; or the coalition may ask directly for a meeting. The coalition or an elected official may arrange a town hall meeting and invite the agency director to participate. You may also encourage a reporter to investigate and do a story on the problem your community has identified.

A more formal way to encourage change is to file an administrative petition. Many states give the public the right to petition agencies to request the adoption, amendment, or repeal of a rule. Also, Congress has given the public the right to petition federal agencies. Using these rights, advocates have filed administrative petitions to bring about important reforms.

Considerations: To get a government agency to solve or prevent a problem, you must convince agency officials that there is a serious problem, that they are responsible for solving or preventing it, and that they can take meaningful steps to implement a viable solution.

Community members sometimes may view the agency itself as the problem. Nonetheless, it is almost always a good idea to talk to agency decision makers once you've gathered your information, done your analysis, and pulled together your supporters. If you are unsuccessful and have to try another strategy, you can make the point that "We tried to work with the agency, but it refused to protect our community. That is why we have come here to [court, the legislature, city council, etc.] for action."

Pluses

- Filing an administrative petition is a formal action that is taken seriously by agency officials and the media.
- Since agencies typically have broad authority to act in the public interest, the petitioning process can address identified problems.
- Petitioners do not have to be represented by lawyers.
- The administrative petitioning process—from filing to agency action—can be fairly short (a few months, rather than the years sometimes required for a lawsuit).
- Depending on the issue, petitioning may be less swayed by political or vested interests than the legislative process is. Moreover, friendly legislators can still help your cause before the agency by voicing their support.
- Administrative petitions may be filed at any time, can request immediate action in an emergency, and can address problems statewide or locally.

Minuses

- Since most agency heads are appointed by the executive branch (typically by governors or mayors) and are subject to oversight by the legislature, they are subject to political pressure.
- Because of their backgrounds, agency heads and staff members may be sympathetic with the industry or profession they are responsible for regulating.
- The legislative branch may sometimes have expressly limited an agency's power over a specific practice or type of entity.

For more in-depth information about the administrative petitioning process and working with administrative agencies, consult *Advocating for Change*, "Administrative Petitioning: Making Rules Stronger," at **www.policylink.org**, and Harry Snyder's *Getting Action: How to Petition Government and Get Results* (San Francisco: Consumers Union, 2003).

Going to Court

Another way to bring about change is to file a lawsuit. In a lawsuit, the plaintiff must do more than simply argue that what the defendant is doing is wrong or harmful. A lawsuit contends that the defendant's actions violate the law. Typically, lawsuits are brought either to stop actions that violate existing laws or to implement actions that are required by them.

Considerations: Community members may sometimes feel that taking a matter to court is necessary to show that the community is strong and is forcefully pursuing its rights and the need for equitable treatment. Sometimes decision makers agree with what you are trying to achieve but because of political considerations want the courts to force them to act.

When agency officials or business executives are sued, they may feel attacked or betrayed, become angry and defensive, and refuse to deal with you except through their lawyers. Because this is a typical reaction, consider other approaches before going to court.

Pluses

- A lawsuit can be filed any business day of the year.
- Plaintiffs can ask for an emergency order or injunction to prevent irreparable harm.
- Courts may be less overtly political than other venues. (However, the election of judges is becoming more politicized and their appointment by elected officials can also become politically charged.)
- A lawsuit can result in an important legal precedent that leads to reforms in other areas.
- In some types of cases, there is the potential for recovering lawyer's fees and costs of litigation.

Minuses

- It is difficult for courts to address matters of pure policy. Judges can't issue orders simply on what they think is best for the public. They are supposed to interpret and enforce existing laws only.
- Unless sufficient funding is available, your lawyer will have to be willing to work pro bono or for a contingent or reduced fee.
- Once a suit is filed, the focus tends to shift to the court and the lawyers, making it harder for members of the community to be involved.
- A well-funded defendant can use tactics that drive up costs in an effort to exhaust a plaintiff's funds.
- Lawsuits can take a long time—sometimes years—especially if there are appeals.

Changing the Law

Another means of bringing about change is to try to persuade the state legislature, city council, or county board of supervisors either to pass a new law or to change an existing one.

Considerations: The legislator (assemblyperson, senator, city councilmember) who agrees to carry your proposed legislation must have the credibility, time, energy, and staff to get it passed and signed into law. She or he should want to be the champion of your issue. The law must meet the community's needs, not just the legislator's political needs. If passed, the law should bring meaningful change and result in, if not a full solution to the problem, a significant step forward.

Pluses

- Legislators and local legislative officials are elected and therefore accountable to voters.
- In smaller communities, elected officials may be easily accessible to members of the public.
- Unlike the courts, the legislature can look beyond existing law and broadly examine public policy to find the best solution.
- A law enacted by the state legislature may address a problem in communities statewide.
- A law enacted by a city council can be a model for other localities and may even pave the way for state legislation. Likewise, a new law enacted by one state legislature can be a model for other states.

Minuses

- Drafting and passing legislation is a highly political process. Elected officials will weigh how their actions will affect their standing with voters, campaign contributors, and supporters.
- In many states, the state legislature is in session for only part of the year or may convene for only a few months every two years. Deadlines for introducing bills and for proposed bills to make their way through the legislative process also put constraints on timing for introduction and passage of measures.
- Legislative rules typically make it easier to block proposed laws or ordinances than to pass them.
- Elected officials like to please everyone, which makes it more difficult to pass controversial legislation.

- The state capital may be so far from your community that it is difficult for community leaders and supporters to meet with legislators and attend hearings there.

Creating Your Own Forum

You may have to create your own forum to focus public attention on an issue. For example, if filing a lawsuit, going to the legislature, or filing an administrative petition is not feasible, you might explore whether a respected local organization or institution (e.g., the NAACP, National Urban League, newspaper, community clinic, church, or union) would sponsor a public hearing on the issue. Ideally, the sponsoring institution will work closely with community leaders to schedule the hearing; invite speakers, elected officials, policymakers, and the media; plan the agenda; and convene and chair the hearings.

Other possibilities include:

- Establishing an organization to focus community and public attention;
- Having candidates focus and comment on your issue during the election season;
- Asking investigative reporters to write articles about your issue;
- Engaging in public actions or protests;
- Developing an issue-oriented website; and
- Persuading elected officials to introduce and pass resolutions calling for action.

Considerations: The success of your forum will typically be judged by the number of people who turn out, the influence of the participants, and the tenor of the event. You are asking the media and the public to pay attention to your event, so a lot of planning and organizing is essential to present the best possible case. You want to counter the notion that you are holding your own event because you have neither community nor official support.

Pluses

- Community leaders have lots of input into aspects of the hearing, including subject matter, how issues will be presented, and who will be invited.
- Organizing a public event can utilize the community's resources and build its capacity to advocate for itself.
- A carefully planned and well-conducted hearing can educate government officials, local politicians, reporters, and the public about your particular problem.
- Public officials can be called on for their views. They may be given the opportunity to tell those attending the hearing what action (if any) they plan to take to address the problem.
- You can schedule your forum when you need to highlight the issue, involve the community, and engage policymakers.

Minuses

- The logistics can be daunting: Community leaders and the sponsoring institution will have to decide where and when to hold the hearing; whether the facility can safely accommodate the number of persons expected; what the tone of the hearing should be; who should be invited to attend; who should chair the hearing; how it should be opened; who should be invited to speak, in what order, and for how long; and how to control speakers who try to dominate or divert it.
- Scheduling a hearing and inviting people to attend is easy. Actually getting them to prepare, attend, and participate in a manner that will result in an effective hearing requires lots of one-on-one effort.
- Holding a public hearing is not an end in itself. It should set the stage for other actions, including legislation, litigation, petitioning administrative agencies, and working with private businesses to bring about change. Be ready to take the next steps.
- Be careful that you don't engage in activities that are prohibited for nonprofits. If your event includes candidates running for office, give all candidates equal opportunity

to attend and speak. Nonprofits should never support or oppose a political candidate and should avoid even the appearance of doing so. It's a fine line: make sure you know the rules so that you do not cross it. Many publications and organizations provide detailed information on the do's and don'ts of nonprofit advocacy. A recommended place to start is The Alliance for Justice at **www.allianceforjustice.org/nonprofit/index.html** or call 202/822-6070.

Choosing the Right Advocacy Strategy

Which advocacy strategy is best will depend on the solution and goals you want to achieve, the resources available to you, the kind of opposition you expect, who the decision makers are, and how receptive they will be to your arguments. You will also need to consider how much time each process will take.

There will be other questions. Is the coalition more comfortable starting off by talking to the company or public official before creating public pressure? Is there an imminent risk, one requiring immediate strong action, like a public demonstration? Can you keep up with the work to handle the follow-through steps if the strategy is to present your facts and arguments at meetings and hearings in the state capital? If you go to court, will the coalition have to take a back seat to lawyers? Will the coalition be perceived as weak if you don't go to court?

Sometimes using more than one strategy can increase pressure, can maintain momentum and media and public interest, and can enhance your organizing and coalition building. Successful campaigns often require coordinated work in more than one forum at a time. Thus, it is essential that the work in different forums be well planned and coordinated so that scarce resources are efficiently used, decision makers are held accountable, and the campaign presents a focused and forceful presence. Choosing the right strategy is difficult. Take your time to carefully think and talk through the options. When you want more information on any specific strategy or additional guidance on factors to consider in your decision, you can consult the PolicyLink online advocacy manual, *Advocating for Change* (**www.policylink.org**). You will learn as you go and refine your own sense of priorities and key decision factors for choosing one strategy over another.

CASE STUDY: For Battered Women

Eva Jefferson Paterson is a renowned civil rights attorney who has been fighting for justice for more than 30 years as a legal aid lawyer, cofounder of the California Coalition for Civil Rights, the Executive Director of the Lawyers' Committee for Civil Rights in San Francisco, and now as the founder and president of the Equal Justice Society. This story, in her own words, is about an early victory she was able to achieve through litigation for the rights of battered women.

⟨⟨⟩⟩

In the fall of 1975, I graduated from law school at the University of California; I had been admitted through its affirmative action program. I went to work for the Legal Aid Society of Alameda County, Oakland, California, and was the first African-American attorney many of my African-American clients had ever seen. Some were delighted. Others asked for a "real" attorney.

The attorneys there saw clients at a drop-in clinic, clients who often had many legal problems. I soon spotted a pattern. Almost every day, black women came in complaining about being beaten by their boyfriends or husbands. These sisters told me that they rarely received any police protection. Many times the police simply did not come when called. If they did come, some officers told the women that they had to get a Temporary Restraining Order (TRO) because this was a civil matter. Police, who were shown a TRO, told the women that the document was meaningless. Some officers advised the woman to walk around the block and then left. Even worse, some officers sided with the batterers and threatened to arrest the women!

This situation seemed wrong to me. Other female attorneys and law clerks were similarly outraged at this pattern; we called it "arrest avoidance." This was in the early days when there was little public discussion about the scourge of domestic violence, so we initially thought these women, because they were black, were not being protected by the police, and that this was a case of race-based discrimination. We assumed white women received help from the police. We soon learned that women of *all* races were being beaten and ignored. Race and social class had nothing to do with this. Women around the city and indeed around the world were being beaten. We learned that a woman was beaten every 18 seconds in this country. Every 18 seconds!!!!

Armed with our law degrees and youthful fearlessness, we sued the Oakland Police Department for violation of the Constitution's guarantee of equal protection under the law. Our case was surrounded by blessings, good omens, and synchronicity. The day we filed the case, I was grocery shopping and noticed a striking graphic on the cover of *Ms.* magazine. It was a woman with a black eye; the issue was devoted to the topic of domestic violence.

Our case, *Scott v. Hart*, was particularly challenging because the U. S. Supreme Court was making it harder and harder to prevail in civil rights cases. In fact, in the case, *Rizzo v. Goode* (Rizzo being Frank Rizzo, the notorious police chief in Philadelphia), hurdles were erected that made it very difficult to win our case. When the attorneys went into the chambers of the judge, he had *Rizzo v. Goode* open on the table in front of him. We were certain we were going to lose. We later learned that the judge's law clerk, a woman, had encouraged him to keep the case alive, which he did. Over the course of the next several years, we were able to convince the powers that be in the Oakland Police Department that the "arrest avoidance" policy was unconscionable.

Ultimately, we settled the case with the Oakland Police Department and got it to agree to eliminate its "arrest avoidance" policy. Though batterers would not be taken into custody the first time they hit someone, those who kept beating women would be arrested. We initiated training for all the police supervisors so that they would learn and follow proper procedures. We wrote a comprehensive plan for handling these calls that was used around the country. The city also contributed $5,000 to help start A Safe Place, a shelter for battered women in Oakland.

After our case, similar cases and challenges were pursued around the country; today, while the system is not perfect, domestic violence is taken seriously by police departments.

About 20 years after we filed *Scott v. Hart*, a local law school invited me to be part of a panel composed of women talking about their careers. As I was describing this litigation, I had an "Aha!" moment. I had a very strong memory that my Mom had been battered. As a skinny seven-year-old, I had tried to protect her from my Dad, but I was too little to do so. We were also a military family, so my Mom would not have felt comfortable calling the military police on my Dad. As I talked to the law students, I realized that this case was brought to protect my Mom retroactively.

We do social justice work for many reasons. This time, protecting my clients meant acknowledging the fact that there had really been no one to protect my Mom.

Communicating a Clear and Compelling Story

Regardless of the venue or forum, your campaign will need to influence the public and decision makers. With broad support and lots of public attention, a just cause can be more powerful than lots of money and political contacts. The challenge is to craft a way to communicate your concerns and goals so that they are understood, are credible, and move people to take action to support you. The three foundations for successful communications strategies are:

- Your information must be accurate;
- You must present your issue in the context of a broadly acknowledged value; and
- You must tell a simple and compelling story.

Using accurate information and reasoned analysis is important for the credibility of your campaign. Your credibility will affect your ability to organize and build a coalition. It will also affect how the public, the media, and decision makers view you. It will be harder to earn support if you exaggerate or omit essential facts.

A broadly acknowledged value may be one as direct as providing safe and affordable housing, or creating more jobs, or reducing the number of children suffering from asthma. Anyone, from any viewpoint, will support an effort related to improving communities if it is clearly stated. There may be differences about whether a specific solution is feasible, affordable, adequate, or fair, but your campaign will have the broadest possible support if the underlying cause is based on a broadly acknowledged value. If the value is indisputable, those who oppose your campaign will need to come up with other solutions rather than simply defeat the proposed solution.

The facts and values are the foundations for telling a simple and compelling story. The real people and institutions that have been or will be affected complete the picture. Successful campaigns are built on and fueled by making a case that people can understand, relate to, and want to see solved.

Establish the Problem

Concentrate first on establishing that there is a problem, what it is, and who is being affected before proposing a particular solution. Until you have communicated in a clear and convincing way that a problem exists, the public, the media, and decision makers will not give credence to or may even be confused by a discussion of how to solve it. If you tell a simple and compelling story, people will want to find a solution.

You can build support for your campaign by talking directly to individuals, groups, opinion leaders, and decision makers as well as by using the media and the Internet. Whatever method you use, your goal is to convince the audience to support your advocacy.

Talk with People

You can educate and convince individuals in many ways that a problem exists about which they should care. Think through who is likely to be affected by the problem and where you can meet and talk with them. By talking to individuals one on one, you will find out what facts and arguments are important to them. Use these conversations to garner support and gather information to present your case in the most effective way.

A good deal of organizing and coalition building is done by getting the message out person to person through house and block meetings, door-to-door canvassing, or passing out information in front of supermarkets and at flea markets. In some communities, church meetings, passing out or posting one-page flyers, talking to youth groups, or visiting senior centers are productive ways to reach people. One project to address domestic violence sent organizers to self-service laundries to reach women in the community to find out their views, experiences, and needs. It worked. An effective program was developed.

Communicate with Opinion Leaders and Decision Makers

Direct communication with opinion leaders and decision makers is crucial to building support for your position and persuading people with the power to act on your behalf. An opinion leader might be a person respected and looked to for leadership in his or her community, such as the director of a local program, a religious leader, or an elected official. These influential people can play a leadership role in your campaign or add weight to your effort. For example, an opinion leader may be the right person to lead or be the spokesperson for the coalition, giving more visibility and importance to your coalition and helping convince others to join in.

You also want to communicate with the decision makers; i.e., the people who can take the action you need to address the problem. You need to find out who will influence or decide your issues. They may be government staff, corporate executives, or elected officials. Once you find out who the key people are, arrange to meet with them.

Key Information

Common Ways to Reach the Media

News releases. A news release tells the story of what is wrong, who says so, and what should be done. News releases are usually no more than two pages and are a good way to keep reporters and editors up to date on the progress of the campaign and important events.

News conferences. At news conferences, people supporting your position talk to reporters about the facts and analysis of the problem and its solution. The speakers have an opportunity to explain data, describe who is being hurt, and why the proposed solution will work. The purposes of the campaign can be laid out, members of the coalition can be introduced, and reporters can ask questions. News conferences should be reserved for significant events.

Talking to reporters and editors. It is important to call and meet with the people who decide if your campaign is newsworthy and how it will be covered. These conversations give you a chance to find out what journalists think about what you are doing. It also gives you a chance to find out what others are saying about your campaign.

Contacting editorial writers. You can try to get a newspaper or other media source to publicly support your position and urge the action you seek. You need to present your facts and analysis with other supporting documents and be prepared to talk to editorial writers either over the phone or in person.

Letters to the editor. You can respond to any related event reported in a newspaper by writing a short letter to the editor with your comments. This can be a reminder to the public and others concerned about the issue and the need for your solution.

Writing an opinion piece. Newspapers—both print and online—and some radio and TV stations will carry a well-thought-out essay describing your issue and views. You may want to contact the opinion editor to discuss whether she or he might be interested in an essay or article. You can check with the newspaper's or station's website for information about length, how to submit it, and contact information.

When you communicate with decision makers, you want to be prepared with information and analysis and have strong supporters from your coalition with you. Whether at a lunch meeting, an office visit, or a formal hearing, your presentation should be carefully planned. Before the meeting, decide on:

- The purpose of the meeting;
- The main points to discuss;
- How to clearly describe the problem;
- What papers or materials you will bring;
- Who will lead your group at the meeting;
- Who will speak, on what points, and in what order; and
- What your group will ask for.

When meeting with decision makers, stick to the facts. Do not overstate the problem or use inflammatory rhetoric. Assume that once the decision makers are convinced of the seriousness of the issue, your sincerity, and the feasibility of your proposed solutions, they will want to help solve the problem. Media coverage can help show opinion leaders and decision makers that you are working on an important issue that the public cares about and that their steps to solve it will be noticed.

Involve the Media

Coalitions use the news media to inform the public about their campaign, mobilize support, and pressure decision makers to act. Most news stories result from hard work to reach and educate reporters and editors. Getting free ("earned") media rather than buying an advertisement for your cause enables you to reach a lot of people at once and demonstrates that the problem you are working on and your proposed solution are important. Elected officials, their staffs, the courts, government agency staffs, leaders of nonprofit agencies, and business leaders pay close attention to the news and editorial commentary as gauges of public interest and the need and possibilities for reform. Public officials are far more reactive than proactive. The media are a powerful tool to help convince decision makers that they need to act and that they should endorse your proposed solution.

Key Information

Will the Media Pay Attention?

Media coverage is an essential element for a successful advocacy campaign. The media cover some issues; others are largely ignored. Following are some questions to ask to determine whether you are likely to get media coverage.

- Is this an interesting and important story, showing evidence of serious problems that endanger individuals and the community?
- Are there credible spokespersons who can describe the problem and people who can talk about the effect on individuals, the community, and the public at large?
- Is it an ongoing problem? Has there been any news coverage of it?
- Have there been similar problems in other areas?
- How have the media covered other complaints about this issue?

The answers to these questions will help assess how much media coverage you can expect. Getting the media to cover a new issue takes time and personal attention. Reporters need to gain an understanding of the problem and be convinced that the time is right for writing or talking about an issue.

CASE STUDY: Defeat of Prop 54 Is a Win for Innovative Communications Strategy

When Proposition 54 qualified for the California ballot, many equity advocates were concerned. The initiative would have banned the collection of data on race, ethnicity, and gender for any efforts receiving state support, including those associated with housing and other infrastructure expenditures. Proposition 54 followed a string of California ballot measures on race-based topics. Equity advocates had tried in 1996 to defeat Proposition 209, which outlawed affirmative action in public institutions, as well as had tried two years earlier in Proposition 187, which sought to limit undocumented immigrants' access to basic services. Advocates brought the lessons learned and the alliances built from these failed attempts to the fight against Proposition 54.

A strong coalition of civil rights, labor, health, and community-based groups formed the Coalition for An Informed California. The groups organized their constituencies and used print, broadcast, and electronic media to galvanize the public and defeat Proposition 54. Campaign organizers invested heavily in research to determine the potential impact of passage of the ban and conducted polls and focus groups to determine messages that would resonate with different communities across the state.

When it became clear that the public was very concerned about the ramifications of virtually eliminating the ability of health researchers to understand and study race and gender-associated diseases, the campaign focused its primary media messages and messengers on this theme. The campaign was able to secure the well-respected and well-known Dr. C. Everett Koop, former Surgeon General of the United States, as a spokesperson opposing the initiative.

The campaign also developed and implemented an Internet strategy that allowed people to sign on to the campaign, enhancing the coalition's ability to build a database of progressive individuals. A flash animation piece was developed with "mainstream" messages about the dangers of failing to collect racial and ethnic data. In addition, three different flash pieces targeting Asian, Latino, and African-American communities were developed. The targeted flash pieces proved particularly potent, with many recipients forwarding the message on to friends, colleagues, and family—at far higher rates than the "mainstream" flash piece was forwarded.

As part of the campaign's paid media strategy, advertisements were purchased on African-American radio and Spanish-language television. Campaign allies also purchased advertisements in ethnic print media, and grassroots organizing efforts included more traditional efforts such as community outreach and education and distributing bumper stickers and "No on Prop 54" flyers.

In the end, Prop 54 was defeated. The huge push to gather support from across the state—a push that incorporated new technology but that was also explicit about reaching California's broad array of racial and ethnic groups—proved to be the key components of success.

Using the Internet

The Internet is an efficient and inexpensive way to reach your supporters, the public, the media, decision makers in government, and corporations. With a little extra effort, the Internet can also be used for fundraising. The two main tools of Internet advocacy are e-mail and websites. You can use e-mail to educate and enlist new supporters to your campaign, to communicate with coalition members, and to communicate with other campaign members by personal mail, discussion forums, and action alerts.

A website can be a powerful tool for communicating your campaign goals, plans, information on how to get involved, how to contact and contribute to the campaign, how and when to contact decision makers, and when to appear at meetings, rallies, and hearings. A website provides the media and policymakers initial access to your campaign and a way to follow up and contact you directly for more information.

The Internet enhances and expands your campaign's communications, which are essential to advocacy. It is not, however, a substitute for the direct personal contact needed to successfully organize, educate, and persuade supporters, the media, and decision makers.

Remember not to overuse e-mail by inundating your supporters and the media with an outpouring of nonessential information. You also need to be aware that IRS rules for nonprofit advocacy activities also apply to the use of the Internet. (For more guidance, see "E-Advocacy for Nonprofits: The Law of Lobbying and Election-Related Activity on the Net," published by The Alliance for Justice, Washington, DC (**www.afj.org**).) E-mails need not be full of text only. New technologies allow short videos to be transmitted, which can be targeted for different audiences and can be compelling enough that they are sent from reader to reader, sparking a sort of "advocacy virus," spreading information and building support.

To be successful, your campaign must use every available method to tell the story of how existing conditions are hurting people and how they can be improved. The Internet and the tools it provides change and evolve rapidly. Watch for, and learn about, new innovations, and then try them as advocacy tools in your own efforts. Check out the PolicyLink report, *Click Here for Change: Your Guide to the E-Advocacy Revolution*, available at **www.policylink.org/ Projects/eadvocacy/default.html**, for an in-depth look at tools, techniques, and case studies that use the Internet for advocacy.

Key Information

Writing a News Release

The news release can be one to two pages and should be written in a journalistic style that includes quotes from your key spokesperson(s). Make the release as interesting as you possibly can. Connect your concern to issues or stories that are already being covered; to an upcoming event; or to someone who is prominent and well-respected and supportive of your issue. Occasionally, news releases are picked up and published in newspapers almost as originally written, so be sure the release is concise and well written, with contact information clearly identified.

Points to remember:

- Print the release on your letterhead.
- List a contact person, a phone number, and an e-mail address (if there is one).
- Be sure that someone will be available if the media call.
- Include the release date and indicate whether the information is "for immediate release" or "embargoed until [date]." Use the latter if you want the media to not publish the information until the date of your event or announcement.

Send your release to reporters, editors, news directors, and producers after finding out their preferences for fax or e-mail. If you send it via e-mail, cut and paste the release into the body of the e-mail; journalists don't want to risk opening attachments. Develop your media list from media directories and by identifying reporters from local media whom you read, watch, or listen to regularly. Be sure to include ethnic, alternative, and community outlets on your media list.

Follow up sending the release with a phone call. Ask if it was received, if coverage is likely, and if more information would be helpful.

Never Quit

Successful advocacy often requires going from one strategy to another and back again. If you win, you have to make sure that the changes won are implemented. If they aren't, you may have to go to court, city hall, or the legislature; or you may have to petition the responsible government agency to demand action. You may need new allies along the way, which will mean additional organizing, communicating, and building trust.

Your opponents may try to undo any progress you make. If you succeed in getting a new law passed, they may take the issue to the ballot or to the courts. On the other hand, even if you lose a battle, there's always another day, another strategy, another set of circumstances with new opportunities. Through all the ups and downs, successes and setbacks, keep going; advocacy is a powerful force for change. It can help you, your community, and your organization to achieve results.

PART II: BUILDING A FOUNDATION FOR ACTION

The following sections lift up the value of community building and emphasize the importance of communities sharing their knowledge and forming deep and abiding bonds with one another. Gathering the facts and coalition building, as described in Part I, are not always easy tasks to complete. History has shown that people tend to refrain from information sharing and that coalitions can become fractured. The innovative communication tools set forth in Part II are included for you to utilize in connection with the more conventional advocacy strategies presented in Part I to strengthen your community connections, which will thereby strengthen your advocacy efforts. For more information on these tools, visit **www.JamestownProject.org**.

Storytelling/story sharing, Reflective Community Practice, Study Circles, The World Café model, and Citizen Deliberative Councils are all methods that can be combined and used to bridge gaps among generations, foster community learning, create new knowledge, and strengthen relationships. Ultimately, we believe that using these powerful tools will enable you to move your advocacy agenda around *Covenant* priority areas, while fostering inclusion, civic participation, and other American democratic values.

Storytelling/Story Sharing

The technique of storytelling transcends race, class, generations, and other differences and allows people to communicate on common ground through a common story. Storytelling is universal. It has its roots in ancient African societies, and for centuries, people have used stories to entertain and educate as well as to instill values and inspire people to action. Describing storytelling as a new nontraditional approach to advocacy sounds strange, given its historical roots, but in modern times, with the advent of complicated electronic media communications methods, storytelling has become a lost art. Organizers and advocates often overlook the power of the spoken word and of shared experiences as a way of communicating and moving people to action.

The storytelling technique that we encourage is called "story sharing." Story sharing is an exciting activity for family reunions, holiday celebrations, church-related events, or any other community gathering. An element essential to the success of any story-sharing experience is the involvement of a facilitator skilled in basic story development. That person must be capable of guiding your group with tact, creativity, and awareness necessary to control emotional topics. For group members to be able to move through the parts of a story to reach a satisfactory (but not necessarily "happy") ending, the facilitator must be able to demonstrate to your group that there is a template that makes such a structure possible. Likewise, when deciding which topics to use, the facilitator must tailor them to match your group's age, interests, and *The Covenant* agenda.

Your group would arrange chairs in a circle and simply begin to share stories that are relevant to the agreed-upon subject area. The rules are few but are important. Story Circles are marked by a communal feeling of love and respect, so only one member of the group should talk at a time. The group should agree upon an estimated length for each story in advance, though this should remain flexible out of respect to the person sharing the story. You could also engage a recorder to ensure that the stories are captured; you could capture the stories using video or audio recording. One innovative methodology that Jamestown has utilized is employing a graphic artist who literally sketches visual depictions of the stories as they are being told.

Another storytelling technique is one-on-one storytelling, where the storyteller shares a story and the listener captures that story. One-on-one storytelling might be appropriate to archive stories of our elders, wherein they may not be able to attend a community story-sharing session. It might also be appropriate in a situation where the storyteller wants to share the story but may be uncomfortable doing so in a large group. Capture techniques are identical to those utilized in story-sharing circles.

By creating repeated storytelling activities throughout your community, you can use the stories of residents to create shared understanding, which can help to create a basis for a plan of action that can lead to improving the conditions of your communities. Essentially, the seeds for real change are sown as "ordinary citizens" consider their role in mobilizing communities to improve democratic participation and citizen engagement.

"Over the course of the last century, the American culture largely abandoned oral stories and a setting for a collective imaginative experience. Today the norm is for people to be passive viewers, responding to a medium that offers images that are contrived and manipulated to evoke specific responses. Audience imagination is not required but rather their willingness to accept the universal image they are shown.

⤜⤝

Stories are accessible to everyone. They help us enjoy living and tolerate the challenges of daily life. They are our birthright and heritage and our lives are made better because of them."

— Catherine Conant,
Telling & Listening to Stories

Story sharing is not a blanket solution that will solve the problems that plague our communities, but rather a beginning step in which we lay the groundwork for individual and *collective* action. Using story sharing, our communities can seize upon and learn from stories so that every individual feels that his or her voice matters. The inclusiveness of a storytelling gathering creates a space that welcomes feedback and pushes no agenda other than the opportunity to freely voice one's opinion on the subject being uplifted. Story Circles place value on opinions that are not often voiced and shed light on perspectives that are frequently disregarded. The simplicity of this effort is one that is often overlooked as public gatherings of this sort typically take place only when discussing issues of a contentious or political nature. The aim is to uplift the "community" voice within your community and to pave the way for community-driven change around *The Covenant* agenda items.

During June 2006, Jamestown collaborated with the New Haven International Arts & Ideas Festival to provide Story Circles to allow New Haven residents to share their experiences with each other. The series of story-sharing sessions, called "Private Narratives for the Public Good," encouraged discussions that allowed citizens to reflect on their individual experiences in an effort to rethink and reconstruct local democracy and civic participation.

The series culminated in a wrap-up session that included actor and author Hill Harper and John O'Neal, Junebug Productions Artistic Director and founder of the Free Southern Theater—the cultural arm of the civil rights movement. Harper and O'Neal reflected upon themes from festival dialogues and the overall power of using stories as a foundation for social change.

❦

The *Color Line Project* is a performance and community story-collecting project that revitalizes civil rights movement history as a valued and an illuminating context for contemporary issues of race. Artist O'Neal collaborates with a network of local organizations, communities, and artists to present his Junebug Jabbo Jones plays based on the movement. Using Story Circles methodology as a dialogue form, O'Neal and other artists work over several months with local scholars, activists, and partner organizations to collect stories of local people about their involvement in and understanding of the movement. Local artists then work with Junebug artists to move the community's stories to public presentation. Junebug's plays, presentations of local movement stories, and scholar panels provide varied opportunities for facilitated public dialogues. The project encourages and trains local scholars, activists, and artists to draw upon civil rights movement stories and Story Circle methodology in their own work and to further public dialogue on contemporary issues of racism. The project could certainly be used to provide a community-determined framework around public dialogue on *Covenant* agenda items.

Reflective Community Practice

Reflective Community Practice is a method of group communication designed to further group thinking and reflecting on collective work and to help organizations ask and answer questions that will lead to aligning their actions with their values and goals. It is closely related to storytelling because it utilizes storytelling as a tool to engage a group in collective discourse and sharing their experiences. In a reflection group, each person might take a turn recounting a key event and getting feedback on analyzing it, naming assumptions, making connections, and formulating critical questions that emerge. When the group engages in collective dialogue about the event or key question, it builds an understanding of a question or an event and locates the significance of the story in the larger context of their work.

To fully understand Reflective Community Practice, you must first think about the meaning of the word "reflection." Reflection refers to the deliberate process of taking your actions into account, examining them, learning from them, and then adjusting your future behavior in accordance with the lessons learned. It is a natural process that many of us engage in routinely on an individual basis. Reflective Practice simply takes "reflection" one step further and means that an individual creates a deliberate habit or routine around examining his or her own experiences.

Reflective Community Practice is different because it moves this deliberate routine practice from an individual to a collective activity. To make this happen, groups engaging in Reflective Community Practice must share their experiences, perhaps using Story Circles and dialogue, to make sure that everyone internalizes them, and *then* move on to examining these collective experiences, learning from them, and ultimately adjusting the future direction of the group in accordance with the lessons learned. This process is not as natural to groups as it is to individuals, and the absence of collective reflective practice is often the root cause of group dysfunction.

Reflective Community Practice could certainly be utilized by any group or local organization engaged in addressing *The Covenant* priority issues. It may not be appropriate for the initial stages of organizing and community building. However, it works well in later stages of activism whenever the group needs to "check in" on its activities to ensure that it is advancing and properly aligned with the organization's goals. Jamestown endorses Reflective Community Practice as a methodology to strengthen communities undertaking the advocacy strategies described in Part I of this toolkit. To make this happen, you may need to use a facilitator trained in Reflective Community Practice. For more information, visit the website of the Center for Reflective Community Practice, **http://crcp.mit.edu**.

Ceasar McDowell is a leading practitioner and scholar in community building and reflective practice. He is one of the founding board members of The Algebra Project, the first Full Professor of the Practice of Community Building at MIT, and Director of MIT's Center for Reflective Community Practice. He is the CEO of the organization, *dropping knowledge international*. In this essay McDowell reveals how his personal journey led to his understanding of the power of voice in reshaping the world.

I believe in the power of reflection, of sharing our stories, and of collectively learning from our past experiences. I believe that these simple, but often overlooked, concepts are so powerful that they can change the lives of individuals and communities alike. I believe that when people become truly engaged with their inner selves and connected to their communities, they will become inspired and empowered to evaluate, change, and improve their current conditions.

I believe in these ideas so passionately that five years ago I started The Center for Reflective Community Practice at the Massachusetts Institute of Technology (MIT). One of the methodologies that I pioneered at the Center is called Critical Moments Reflection (CMR). Essentially, CMR helps people reflect on their past experiences.

Ironically, reflecting on my own past helped me cultivate CMR as a practice. I am part of the first generation in our extended family to be born and raised outside of the rural South. Each summer I would leave the ethnically complex neighborhood of East Denver to visit my grandparents in a little rural community in the Louisiana delta, which until the 1960s did not have the luxury of running water.

While the difference between the rural and urban was stark, these communities actually had a lot in common. Close relationships and the importance of family, friends, and neighbors shaped both environments. Both communities were also shaped by their relatively limited access to "power" and economic resources. Both were full of inventiveness and self-sufficiency. And the ability to "make do" defined both communities because it was in the soul and body of the people who inhabited these two places.

As I reflected on these experiences, another similarity between the two places plagued me. It was striking how infrequently people talked about the fullness of their lives and the story of how they managed to live, survive, and in many cases thrive in a world that was hostile to them. Many people in both communities were functionally illiterate, rendering them functionally voiceless. They could read to make their way through everyday life and speak to negotiate the daily necessities of life. But they could not write nor speak their experiences of the world. Nor could they read the words of others who were trying to find their truth in the world. The inadequacy of personal and community reflection would continue to haunt me profoundly for years to come. This is where my journey began.

As the Director of the Center at MIT, I have had the privilege of seeing Critical Moments Reflection work firsthand and watch it enable individuals and groups to uncover or create knowledge from their own experiences for improving their future actions. The CMR methodology leads groups of people through a reflective process that helps them to step back from their experiences, review their understanding of those experiences, and draw lessons that they can use to improve their future actions or work. The goal of the CMR process is to enable individuals and groups to uncover or create knowledge from their own experiences for improving their future actions.

Just prior to writing this essay, I was in San Salvador, attending a Knowledge Fair that the MIT Center had co-designed. Of course we had infused the principles of the CMR process, including reflection and story sharing into the fair's design. During the fair, El Salvadorians from poor rural communities exchanged what they had learned from their local efforts to overcome poverty. They displayed projects that they had undertaken on their own and openly discussed with over 1,000 fair-goers how their projects worked, what they understood about themselves, and their respective views about the effects of poverty that allowed them to create their projects. By participating in the Knowledge Fair, community members had crystallized questions they may have had about their work, while simultaneously sharing their stories and increasing collective community knowledge. They also confirmed what I had already believed with certainty—the fact that at the heart of this work of uncovering local knowledge is the art of storytelling.

I was especially humbled and gratified on the last day of the Knowledge Fair when a person came up to me and said, "Thank you for what you have done. I have worked with these communities for many years, but it was not until we used the process you designed that they were able to see the value of their own efforts and the richness of their own knowledge. You have given us a great gift that will help sustain us into the future." That moment encapsulated for me the power of people rediscovering their own voice. It is the complexity of these individual stories and the way in which they meld together to create community connections that show us the way to positively support the ability of all people to ensure that they have a just, safe, and healthy life.

My experience in El Salvador was just one of many that have shown me that people all over the world want a way to give voice to their experiences in the world and to share their stories with the world in order to create the possibility of changing the world. Toward this end, in 2006 I took on the leadership of an international organization called *dropping knowledge international.* Its purpose is to harness the power of communications technology and the Internet to make it possible for people from around the world to raise the questions they have about making the world a fairer, safer, and more just place. One way we do this is through convening the Table of Free Voices®, in which 112 people gather in public at a round table to answer questions that the collective public has deemed vital to the world.

Through dropping knowledge international, we are attempting to do on a global scale what veteran civil rights leader Bob Moses said was so important for the movement in Mississippi. When asked about the most important thing to emerge out of the civil rights struggles in Mississippi, Moses said simply, "the meeting." What Moses recognized then is that the voices, insights, and knowledge of sharecroppers who lived through the consequences of oppression were essential to understanding, overcoming, and reshaping the conditions that created their oppression. Dropping knowledge international provides the opportunity for oppressed people around the world to share their voices, insights, and knowledge. Through this process, dropping knowledge international quite literally can change the world.

And it is no accident that my own personal reflection confirms the criticality of this methodology of reflection and story sharing. My story has confirmed for me that the failure to provide a venue that allows these voices to be heard can be deadly. My father died of kidney failure brought on by hypertension. On one level I tell myself that his hypertension was directly related to the life he led as a black man of his generation desperately longing for change. But I also firmly believe that if he had a venue where his voice could have been heard and respected in the world, much of that stress and tension would have not been confined to his body, allowing him to lead a longer, healthier life.

Today in our communities, the tensions of being black in this country and in the world are often expressed through violence, neglect, and indifference. We inflict violence upon those we love and often against members of our community whom we don't even know. We neglect our children, our neighborhoods, and, most tragically, ourselves, demonstrating a heinous indifference for our individual and collective future. How different it would be if we as black people invested in learning how to give voice to our experiences in all their complexities. How different it would be if we then made space to listen to and learn from each other with a deep abiding sense of love. The difference is between survival and extinction, and the choice is ours to make. Choose love.

Asking Questions

Simple yet profound, the art of effective questioning is another, often overlooked mode of communication to promote community action. Indeed, asking questions has formed the foundation for social change for centuries. In 1851, Sojourner Truth asked, "Ain't I a Woman?" That humble question spurred the abolitionist and suffrage movements and still today fosters the basis for inclusion of black and brown women in the women's movement. A full century later, Nelson Mandela questioned racial segregation in South Africa and fueled the anti-apartheid movement through his ultimate ascension to his country's presidency in 1994. When citizens fail to ask questions, the result is the kind of dangerous acquiescence that nurtured an environment where Hitler would rise to power, or where the barbarities of the African slave trade could be overlooked as justifiable. A society's failure to question its leaders and its government can lead to dangerous outcomes.

This section uplifts "asking questions" as a mode of communication that can open the door to knowledge and understanding. In particular, we explore utilizing the wide reach of the Internet to unleash this modest but powerful tool. Utilizing this technology can broadly expand your ability to reach volumes of people who can contribute to and inform community questioning around *Covenant* priority issues.

To launch an effective "asking questions" campaign, a small group of organizers would prepare a list of the subjects around which you would like your community to ask questions. Your community's *Covenant* priority issues would guide subject matter. Once the parameters are defined, you would launch your campaign utilizing any means necessary to get the broadest input in developing a list of questions. You would e-mail everyone in your community. You would knock on doors. You would stand outside of the grocery store and post office. You would strike up conversations with the garbage men; the parking enforcement officers; the elderly men playing checkers in the park; and homeless men, women, and children. You would use video tape, audio tape, a laptop computer, or a pen and paper to capture their thoughts and ideas on profound questions they would like answered around *The Covenant* priority areas. For innovative ideas around creating a question campaign, visit the dropping knowledge international website, **www.droppingknowledge.org**.

Once you have enough input, you would sort and categorize the questions. Obtaining "answers" to the questions is the interesting part. You could convene a community meeting, present them to your elected officials, or send them to your local newspaper. Regardless of what you do with them, the important point here is the *process* of the community asking questions in the first place. Here the process and the community participation dispel the myth of community apathy.

Study Circles

The technique mentioned earlier in this book that was used in Peoria, Illinois, to advance *The Covenant* goals was "Study Circles," voluntary adult education groups of five to 20 people who meet three to six times to explore a subject. Each meeting usually lasts two to three hours and is directed by a moderator whose role is to foster a lively but focused dialogue. Because Study Circles are often formed to examine crucial social issues, we think that these circles lend themselves completely to communities or organizations that are preparing to take action on *Covenant* agenda items. In particular, organizations interested in implementing *The Covenant* Curriculum Manual & Study Guide can easily do so utilizing a Study Circle model.

To launch a Study Circle, first visit the website of the Study Circle Resource Center, **www.StudyCircles.org**, where you will find a wealth of information that communities can use to develop their own ability to solve problems by bringing lots of people together in dialogue. Visit the "What Communities Do" section of this site to find a toolkit that will guide you through the process. The materials the group uses will vary. To address *Covenant* priority items, you should download information from **www.covenantwithblackamerica.com**, your online portal to commence engaging around these issues. You can also contact the Study Circle Resource Center, as it can provide you with ready-made materials on various issues, such as Education, Neighborhoods and Families, Police-Community Relations, and Criminal Justice that mirror *The Covenant* priority issues.

Remember, the characteristics of Study Circles are that they are small, voluntary, democratic, and "non-expert." They encourage people to formulate their own ideas about issues and to share them with others. This process helps ordinary people overcome their sense that they lack information or that they are somehow inadequate to engage in and try to solve complex problems. Because of their powerful ability to educate and activate people, Study Circles are used by millions of people today. In fact, in Sweden—where this process is perhaps most popular—the government funds Study Circles in recognition of their usefulness in developing solutions to complex issues pressing upon cities and towns. The Jamestown Project endorses the Study Circle process as we inspire communities to operationalize the *Covenant with Black America*. We emphasize that it is particularly compatible with implementing *The Covenant* Curriculum Manual & Study Guide. We welcome your community's feedback if you decide to utilize this cutting-edge communications technique as you take action on *The Covenant* agenda items that your community cares about most.

The World Café

The World Café is a process of organizing multiple conversations so that they connect, generate knowledge, and cement new relationships. Designed by Juanita Brown, Ph.D., and David Isaacs, it will enable you to create a welcoming environment where participants can learn from one another, recognize innovative insights, and emerge focused and ready to address *Covenant* priority issues. The World Café began only 12 years ago in the living room of its creators, yet today hundreds of thousands of people in corporations, nonprofit organizations, governments, and educational institutions have engaged in Café conversations on six continents.

If you are interested in hosting a Café conversation, you must first consider if it is right for you, particularly as you embark on addressing *The Covenant* agenda with your community or organization. It is particularly useful when people need to engage in authentic conversation, whether they are meeting for the first time or tackling a difficult issue. It is also useful when you want to generate real input, deepen relationships, explore action possibilities around real-life issues, or to create meaningful interaction between a speaker and an audience. Also remember that Café conversations work best with groups larger than 12. Small groups would benefit more from a Study or Story Circle.

To organize a Café conversation, first visit The World Café website, **www.TheWorldCafe.com**. The "Resources" section of this website offers an excellent and a concise guide, "Café to Go," for free. Café to Go guides you step by step so that you can easily adapt your efforts to organize community conversation around *Covenant* priority issues. Essentially, you will organize participants at small Café-style tables with each table having a "host" and a question to be considered. Questions will be determined by *Covenant* agenda items and the community's determination of their priority. After 20 minutes of conversations, table "guests" progress to the next table, leaving the "host" who has taken notes, doodled, and jotted down key ideas. After a few rounds, conversations will become "cross pollinated" with insights from prior conversations. The connections among the ideas shared at these tables and the actions that emerge from this web of conversations will help to build your organization's knowledge base and shape its future.

You can learn more about The World Café by surfing its website and reviewing and purchasing some of the resources available there or by purchasing the book, *The World Cafe: Shaping Our Futures Through Conversations That Matter* (San Francisco: Berrett-Koehler Publishers, 2005), by Juanita Brown, David Isaacs, and The World Café Community. The book is available through both **www.Amazon.com** and **www. BarnesandNoble.com**. As with the previously described approaches, The Jamestown Project believes in The World Café. We think it is a cutting-edge communications technique that will help you take action on your community's *Covenant* priority issues.

Citizen Deliberative Councils

The last of the innovative nontraditional approaches that we highlight in this section is known as Citizen Deliberative Councils (CDCs). CDCs differ from the approaches previously discussed in that they would almost exclusively be utilized when your organization is far beyond the "getting started" stage and well into the stage when you are down to brass tacks advocacy, trying to persuade others to your view. CDCs are temporary, face-to-face councils of a dozen or more citizens who convene typically for two to 10 days to consider a complex issue of great public concern. Council members hear from and can cross-examine experts and also collectively reflect on information gathered with the help of a trained facilitator. Importantly, council members are usually selected at random, with safeguards in place to ensure gender, racial, socioeconomic, and other diversity. After learning and reflection, council members generally craft a statement announcing their findings to the public and relevant officials and agencies.

Ultimately, the CDCs disband, as they have no permanent or official power other than the power of legitimacy inherent in their well-publicized, common-sense solutions to compelling public problems. Hundreds of CDCs have been convened worldwide and have demonstrated that, with this method, ordinary citizens have an extraordinary ability to grapple with complex problems and come up with useful recommendations, helping to make democracy real. To find out more about CDCs and how they can be used creatively, read the article, "Using Citizen Deliberative Councils to Make Democracy More Potent and Awake," by Tom Atlee, which is available in the "Articles" section of the website of the Co-Intelligence Institute, **www.co-intelligence.com**.

CDCs may be a useful strategy for organizations addressing *The Covenant* agenda. Certainly, our agenda items meet the standard of "complex issues of great public concern." Additionally, many of these issues tend to stimulate spirited debate with proponents on one side of the issue distrusting proponents of the other side. Once your organization gets started with putting *The Covenant* into action, if you find yourselves at an impasse with other groups or unable to get enough people in leadership roles to listen, consider a CDC. Suggest that an elected official or perhaps a loosely formed coalition of groups convene a CDC as a potential solution to break the impasse or to get the public to pay attention. The power of the legitimacy that the CDC will have cannot be understated. The Jamestown Project endorses CDCs, and we welcome feedback via *The Covenant* website and through our website, **www.JamestownProject.org**, as to whether this approach proved useful.

Putting It All Together

Successful advocacy is contingent on many factors. For some, success may come with a quick and simple call to an elected community official. It may result from writing a news release or merely notifying media outlets about the particular issue at hand. For most communities, however, successful advocacy can be quite elusive. Groups too often are not deeply connected enough as stakeholders seeking the same improvements for their communities. And too often groups are not reflective enough to learn from past experiences and to adjust their behavior based upon these lessons.

All in all, to be successful advocates for change around *The Covenant* priority areas, communities will have to combine the strategies set forth in Part I of this toolkit with the communications techniques offered in Part II. Remember: an advocate is someone who speaks for or pleads the case for himself or herself or for others. So to be successful community advocates, individuals must deeply connect and fully communicate with their fellow community members around the issues that bind them. It may not be easy. And it may seem like a longer road to travel. But ultimately, we believe that it is a road that will lead to *sustained, coordinated, long-term* action as well as to real and effective change.

Selected Bibliography

- Amulya, Joy, "What is Reflective Practice," The Center for Reflective Community Practice, available at **http://crcp. mit.edu/documents/whatis.pdf**
- Co-Intelligence Institute website, **www.Co-Intelligence.org**
- Conant, Catherine, *Telling & Listening to Stories*
- Dropping knowledge international website, **www.drop pingknowledge.org**
- Study Circle Resource Center website, **www.Study Circles.org**
- The World Café website, **www.TheWorldCafe.com**

A CALL TO ACTION

The year 2007 marks the 400-year anniversary of the founding of the Jamestown settlement—America's earliest democratic society. For African Americans, the occasion is bittersweet. As other Americans celebrate this momentous event that established the foundation for our country's greatness, African Americans are reminded, yet again, that for many of us the promises of democracy are not yet real.

African Americans have lived and died by the democratic ideals that Jamestown represents. There is no greater evidence of this than the mass civic participation that characterized the civil rights movement. We believe in the Jamestown ideals, but for us, Jamestown is inextricably linked with the dehumanizing enslavement of our ancestors. The Transatlantic Slave Trade was brutal and deadly. The number of Africans who died during the Middle Passage is difficult to confirm, but estimates range from four to 25 million. Those who did not perish on the ocean floor lost their history, their language, their legacy, their religion, and knowledge of themselves. For African Americans, the anniversary of the founding of the Jamestown settlement is a cause for soul-searching, not celebration.

Today, four centuries later, we must still answer the question: How do we make the promises of democracy real for African Americans?

This is a Call to Action.

For decades, African Americans like most Americans have been in a self-satisfied slumber. Whether caused by complacency, helplessness, or the ire and bitterness resulting from the legacy of slavery and discrimination, we have not met the challenges of our day with anywhere near the passion, commitment, bravery, and collective action that the civil rights generation summoned to overcome the difficulties it faced.

This is a Call to Action.

In 2006, when the *Covenant with Black America* rose to number 1 on the *New York Times Book Review* Best-Seller List, it was a curious thing. Had Black America begun to wake from its slumber? As evidenced by its swift sales, *The Covenant* and its meteoric rise touched the souls of black folk in America. Our community was hungry for change. *The Covenant* had spawned a movement.

This is a Call to Action.

A covenant is a solemn commitment among a group of people to act in harmony to achieve specific goals. We cannot let the *Covenant with Black America* be yet another conversation that black folk had about the problems confronting the black community. Let us make it a solemn commitment. Let us capitalize and build on *The Covenant* movement. Let us use the momentum that has been created to move our community to places that we have never dreamed or imagined.

This is a Call to Action.

We must take the energy generated by *The Covenant* and strategically move it to *sustained, coordinated, long-term* action. We are the masters of our destiny. We can be the catalysts for dramatic change in our own lives and in the life of our community, daring to believe that we have the power and the ability to change the course of history.

This is a Call to Action.

When we make Black America better, we make *all* of America better.

This is a Call to Action.

And the time to act is NOW.

AFTERWORD
by Cornel West

Tavis Smiley's history-making *Covenant with Black America* was a grand moment in the rich tradition of deep democracy in America. His heroic effort to keep alive the great legacy of Martin Luther King, Jr., contributed to the slow melting of the Ice Age of the present era—an era where it became fashionable to be indifferent to the social misery and economic anxiety of the vulnerable and vincible in American society. The upsurge of new energy in the election of 2006 may constitute a democratic awakening to the obscene wealth inequality led by unaccountable corporate elites—the new aristocracy of our economy—and the corrupt rule of incompetent politicians, the old poll-driven public officials that too often lie, spy, and authorize torture here and abroad. This black-led effort to revitalize American democracy exemplifies our present moment.

But can this *moment* sustain a grassroots *momentum* that truly creates a lasting shift in our priorities from well-financed prisons to quality schools, extravagant CEO salaries to workers' living wages, high-tech cosmetic surgeries to universal healthcare, and fancy strip clubs to formidable civic associations? This follow-up book—THE COVENANT *In Action*—reveals the moral hunger and political thirst of fellow citizens who yearn for a more fair and decent society. It also shows that millions of us are willing to fight for new democratic priorities so that this *moment* generates a solid *momentum* for progressive social change. Our fundamental aim is to create an effective and a compassionate *movement*—of courageous leaders and creative organizations—that lets justice run down like water that flows from a genuine love for and service to others. The sacrificial spirit of Martin Luther King, Jr., must flourish in institutional forms and individual lives.

And let us not be deceived. The American historical record suggests that the black-led struggle against white supremacy—especially against racist effects in our economy, schools, healthcare, and cultural industries—is the most appropriate starting point for democratic revitalization of our society. The gifts of black folk in our time are to convince all of us to muster the courage to think critically, act compassionately, and hope unconditionally for a democratic *moment, momentum,* and *movement* that use the best of our historic roots as springboards for contemporary routes that empower everyday people to expand dignity and decency. This is what Tavis Smiley's *Covenant* project is all about—as Martin Luther King, Jr., smiles from his grave!

APPENDIX I:
THE COVENANT CURRICULUM

On February 25, 2006, "*The Covenant* Curriculum: A Study of Black Democratic Action," co-authored by Princeton professors Cornel West and Eddie Glaude (a Jamestown Board Member and a Founding Member/Senior Fellow, respectively) was unveiled at the annual "State of the Black Union" event sponsored by Tavis Smiley.

The Curriculum provides an impressive reading list that situates black democratic strivings in a larger historical narrative of American democratic strivings. The Curriculum is an excellent outline for "students" and people interested in studying and learning about the history of African-American political participation and social movement mobilization.

Because the proponents of *The Covenant* movement believe that learning and action are two concepts that must remain linked, *The Covenant* Curriculum has been included here as an appendix to inspire learning, research, and increased knowledge.

Using the Curriculum as a foundation, Jamestown has developed "*The Covenant* Curriculum Manual & Study Guide," which explains the readings provided by professors West and Glaude, as well as uniquely designed enrichment activities and cooperative learning strategies for students and community members. The manual collapses the traditionally truncated annual discussion of "black history" and better locates the African-American struggle for freedom within the broader narrative of America's past and continuing struggle to make real the promises of democracy. The Curriculum Manual makes this critical knowledge real and accessible to project participants. If you are interested in delving deeper into these subjects, read "*The Covenant* Curriculum Manual & Study Guide" presented by The Jamestown Project, which may be found at **www.covenantwithblackamerica.com**.

The Covenant Curriculum:
A Study of Black Democratic Action

*[I]t was the rise and growth among the slaves of a determination
to be free and an active part of American democracy that forced
American democracy continually to look into the depths. . . .
One cannot think then of democracy in America or in the
modern world without reference to the American Negro.*

— W.E.B. Du Bois,
The Gift of Black Folk (1924)

Course Description

The struggle for black freedom has been and continues to be the highest form of democratic action in American history. In other words, the black freedom struggle—from abolitionism to contemporary black quests for justice—has been and is the moral and civic conscience of a fragile democratic experiment whose limitations are shaped, in part, by white supremacy. Without the black freedom struggle, American democracy lacks integrity and maturity. To travel the road of black democratic action, then, is to pursue a path of courageous efforts to achieve our country.

The aim of this course is to introduce the student to the complex array of black democratic practices from slavery to our contemporary moment. This will be done by close readings of books, speeches, and images that, in our view, best capture the dynamics of black democratic action—action, we believe, called for in *The Covenant*.

Topics and Readings

Week 1: **The Grand Scholar of Black Democratic Action**

- W.E.B. Du Bois, *The Souls of Black Folk*

Week 2: **Historical Background: The Original Hypocrisy**

- "The Declaration of Independence"
- Thomas Jefferson, "Notes on the State of Virginia," Wilson Jeremiah Moses (ed.), *Classical Black Nationalism: From the American Revolution to Marcus Garvey,* pp. 45–47
- David Walker, *Appeal in Four Articles; Together with a Preamble, to the Coloured Citizens of the World, but in Particular, and Very Expressly, to Those of the United States*
- Deborah Gray White, "Let My People Go: 1804–1860," Robin D.G. Kelley and Earl Lewis (eds.), *To Make Our World Anew: Volume I: A History of African Americans to 1880,* pp.169–226

Week 3: **Slavery: Exploited Labor, Degraded Bodies, and Resilient People**

- Frederick Douglass, *Narrative of the Life of Frederick Douglass*

Week 4: **Slavery and the American Imagination**

- Mark Twain, *The Adventures of Huckleberry Finn*

Week 5: **Prelude to War**

- John Hope Franklin, *From Slavery to Freedom: A History of African Americans* (eighth edition), pp. 192–219
- "First Lincoln-Douglas Debate, Ottawa, Illinois," Andrew Delbanco (ed.), *The Portable Abraham Lincoln,* pp. 97–140
- Frederick Douglass, "July 5th Oration," William L. Andrews (ed.), *The Oxford Frederick Douglass Reader,* pp. 108–130

Week 6: **The Civil War: Hypocrisy Explodes**

- John Hope Franklin, "Civil War," *From Slavery to Freedom: A History of African Americans* (eighth edition), pp. 220–244

- Abraham Lincoln, "The Second Inaugural," Andrew Delbanco (ed.), *The Portable Abraham Lincoln*, pp. 320–321
- Henry Highland Garnet, "Let the Monster Perish," Philip S. Foner (ed.), *Lift Every Voice: African American Oratory, 1787–1900*, pp. 459–497
- Walt Whitman, "When Lilacs Last in the Dooryard Bloom'd," *Whitman: Poetry and Prose* (The Library of America), pp. 459–467

Assignment #1: Black Democratic Action requires personal integrity and historical memory. Therefore all of our work must be informed by moral vision and the power of history. You are charged to write an historical time-line of the black presence in America, from the American Revolution to the end of American slavery. Use dates, images, and music to tell heroic stories.

Week 7: **Reconstruction: A Failed Experiment in Multiracial Democracy**

- Noralee Frankel, "Breaking the Chains, 1860–1880," Robin D.G. Kelley and Earl Lewis (eds.), *To Make Our World Anew: Volume I: A History of African Americans to 1880*, pp. 227–280

Week 8: **The Rise of Jim Crow: American Terrorism Run Amok**

- *The Birth of a Nation* (1915 movie)
- Ida B. Wells, *A Red Record*
- C. Vann Woodward, *The Strange Career of Jim Crow*, pp. 3–96
- James Allen (ed.), *Without Sanctuary: Lynching Photography in America*

Week 9: **New Organizations and Courageous Leadership: Black Democratic Responses to American Terrorism**

- James R. Grossman, "A Chance to Make Good: 1900–1929," Robin D.G. Kelley and Earl Lewis (eds.), *To Make Our World Anew: Volume II: A History of African Americans Since 1880*, pp. 67–130

- T. Thomas Fortune, "It is Time to Call a Halt," Philip S. Foner (ed.), *Lift Every Voice: African American Oratory, 1787–1900*, pp. 713–727
- Mary Church Terrell, "In Union There is Strength," Philip S. Foner (ed.), *Lift Every Voice: African American Oratory, 1787–1900*, pp. 840–845
- Richard Wright, *12 Million Black Voices*

Week 10: **Black Democratic Dreams and Global Realities**

- Robin D.G. Kelley, "The Negro Question: Red Dreams of Black Liberation," *Freedom Dreams: The Black Radical Tradition*, pp. 36–59

Week 11: **White Supremacy and the American Imagination**

- James Baldwin, *The Fire Next Time*

Assignment #2: *Black Democratic Action requires individual courage and collective organization. Therefore all of our work for human dignity and freedom must be informed by the extraordinary efforts of ordinary men and women who served and sacrificed for the precious ideals of democracy. You are charged to find and interview a person in your family or community who was a part of the black freedom movements of the 1960s and 1970s.*

Week 12: **Black Social Movements: Hypocrisy Exposed**

- Manning Marable, *Race, Reform, and Rebellion: The Second Reconstruction in Black America, 1945–1990*, pp. 40–85
- Martin Luther King, Jr., "A Testament of Hope," James Melvin Washington (ed.), *A Testament of Hope: The Essential Writings and Speeches of Martin Luther King, Jr.*, pp. 313–328
- *Eyes on the Prize: America's Civil Rights Years/Bridge to Freedom 1965* (1987 documentary)

Week 13: **Courage, Conviction, and Compassion: Black Youth and Democratic Action**

- Melba Pattillo Beals, *Warriors Don't Cry: A Searing Memoir of the Battle to Integrate Little Rock's Central High*

Week 14: **Black Social Movements II: Hypocrisy Exposed**

- Manning Marable, *Race, Reform, and Rebellion: The Second Reconstruction in Black America, 1945–1990*, pp. 86–113
- Malcolm X, "Not just an American problem, but a world problem," Bruce Perry (ed.), *Malcolm X: The Last Speeches*, pp. 151–181
- *Eyes on the Prize II: America at the Racial Crossroads* (1990 documentary)

Week 15: **Black Democratic Action: The Age of the American Empire**

- Robin D.G. Kelley, "Into the Fire: 1970 to the Present," Robin D. G. Kelley and Earl Lewis (eds.), *To Make Our World Anew: Volume II: A History of African Americans Since 1880*, pp. 265–341
- Imani Perry, "Bling Bling . . . Going Pop," *Prophets in the Hood*, pp. 191–203
- Tavis Smiley, *Covenant with Black America*

Assignment #3: Black Democratic Action requires unshakable determination and creative imagination. Therefore all of our work should not only build on the best of freedom struggles but also envision new ways of challenging and changing the powers that be. You are charged to identify and analyze three towering Hip-Hop artists in light of the principles of black democratic action you have learned in this course.

Additional Web Resources

African-American History (University of Washington Library)
http://www.lib.washington.edu/subject/History/tm/black.html

African-American History and Culture
http://www.loc.gov/rr/mss/guide/african.html

African-American History Digital Library
http://www.academicinfo.net/africanamlibrary.html

Library of Congress
http://memory.loc.gov/ammem/aaohtml/exhibit/aointro.html

The Schomburg Center for Research in Black Culture
http//www.nypl.org/research/sc/sc.html

The Schomburg Collection (Images from/of Harlem)
http://www.si.umich.edu/CHICO/Harlem/

The Schomburg Collection (Images of African Americans in the 19th Century)
http://digital.nypl.org/schomburg/images_aa19

APPENDIX II:
AFRICAN-AMERICAN HISTORY TIMELINE[8]

THE COVENANT *In Action* is being released concurrently with the celebration of the 400th anniversary of the Jamestown (Virginia) settlement, representing the first expression of democracy in the New World. But for African Americans, 1607 does *not* represent a celebration, for they did not arrive on these shores as free people. Their history, their heritage, their legacy were not a part of the record then . . . and for too many black folk today, the record is still not clear.

It is only appropriate, then, that *The Covenant* movement include a history of African Americans to not only understand where we have to go, but—equally importantly—from whence we have come! We believe that the following timeline is both informative and instructive.

---

[8] This African-American history timeline was created by Quintard Taylor, the Scott and Dorothy Bullitt Professor of American History at the University of Washington. A prolific writer, he is the author of *The Forging of A Black Community: Seattle's Central District from 1870 through the Civil Rights Era* (Seattle: University of Washington Press, 1994), and *In Search of the Racial Frontier: African Americans in the America West, 1528–1990* (New York: W.W. Norton, 1998). He is co-editor of *African-American Women Confront the West, 1600–2000* (Norman: University of Oklahoma Press, 2003) and of *Seeking El Dorado: African Americans in California* (Seattle: University of Washington Press, 2001). His work on African-American Western History; African-American, African, Afro-Brazilian, and comparative ethnic history has appeared in numerous journals, among them: *Western Historical Quarterly, Oregon Historical Quarterly, The Annals of the American Academy of Political and Social Science,* and *Journal of Negro History.*

Taylor is on the Board of Trustees of the Northwest African-American Museum in Seattle and The Idaho Black History Museum in Boise. He has taught at universities in Washington, Oregon, California, and Nigeria over his 35-year career. For more information, visit **http://faculty.washington.edu/qtaylor/**.

Timeline: Before 1601

c. 476—End of the Roman Empire.

c. 750—Islam is introduced in West Africa.

c. 800—Evidence suggests that African travelers may have come to the Americas before Europeans. One indication is the great stone carvings of the Olmec era in Mexico, bearing African facial features.

951—Paris is founded.

1076—The Empire of Ghana emerges in West Africa.

1230—The Empire of Mali emerges in West Africa.

1260—By this date the city of Timbuktu is the religious, commercial, and political center of the Empire of Mali.

1400—By this date a flourishing slave trade exists in the Mediterranean World. Most of the slaving countries are Italian principalities such as Florence and Venice. Most of those enslaved are Greeks and Eastern Europeans. Between 1414 and 1423, 10,000 Eastern European slaves are sold in Venice alone.

1434—The Portuguese establish trading outposts along the West African coast.

1441—Antam Goncalvez of Portugal captures Africans in what is now Senegal, initiating direct European involvement in the African slave trade.

1450—The Kingdom of Benin emerges in West Africa.

1453—The Ottoman Turks capture Constantinople and thus divert the trade in Eastern European slaves away from the Mediterranean to Islamic markets. The Italians increasingly look to North Africa as their source for slaves.

1464—The Empire of Songhai emerges in West Africa.

1468—Mali conquered by the Empire of Songhai.

1470—By this point small vineyards and sugar plantations have emerged around Naples and on the island of Sicily with Africans as the primary enslaved people providing the labor on these estates.

1490—Small populations of free and enslaved Africans extend from Sicily to Portugal.

1492—Christopher Columbus makes his first voyage to the New World, opening a vast new empire for plantation slavery.

1494—The first Africans arrive in Hispaniola with Christopher Columbus. They are free persons.

1501—The Spanish king allows the introduction of enslaved Africans into Spain's American colonies.

1511—The first enslaved Africans arrive in Hispaniola.

1513—Thirty Africans accompany Vasco Nunez de Balboa on his trip to the Pacific Ocean.

1517—Bishop Bartolome de Las Casas petitions Spain to allow the importation of twelve enslaved Africans for each household immigrating to America's Spanish colonies. De Las Casas later regrets his actions and becomes an opponent of slavery.

1518—King Charles I of Spain grants the first licenses to import enslaved Africans to the Americas.

The first shipload of enslaved Africans directly from Africa arrives in the West Indies. Prior to this time, Africans were taken first to Europe.

1519—Hernan Cortez begins his conquest of the Aztec Empire. Black Spaniards are among the Conquistadors.

1520s—Enslaved Africans are used as laborers in Puerto Rico, Cuba, and Mexico.

1522—African slaves stage a rebellion in Hispaniola. This is the first slave uprising in the New World.

1526—Spanish colonists led by Lucas Vasquez de Ayllon build the community of San Miguel de Guadape in what is now Georgia. They bring along enslaved Africans, considered to be the first in the present-day United States. These Africans flee the colony, however, and make their homes with local Indians. After Ayllon's death, the remaining Spaniards relocate to Hispaniola.

1527–1539—Esteban, a Moroccan-born Muslim slave, explores what is now the Southwestern United States.

1540—An African from Hernando de Soto's Expedition decides to remain behind to make his home among the Native Americans there.

Africans serve in the New Mexico Expeditions of Francisco Vasquez de Coronado and Hernando de Alarcon.

1542—The Spanish Crown abolishes Indian slavery in its colonial possessions.

1550—The first slaves directly from Africa arrive in the Brazilian city of Salvador.

1562—An expedition to Hispaniola led by John Hawkins, the first English slave trader, sparks English interest in that activity. Hawkins' travels also call attention to Sierra Leone. Hawkins is knighted in 1588 for his service in England's victory over the Spanish Armada.

1565—African farmers and artisans accompany Pedro Menendez de Aviles on the expedition that establishes the community of San Agustin (St. Augustine, Florida).

1570—New Spain's (Colonial Mexico) population includes 20,569 blacks and 2,439 mulattoes.

1573—Professor Bartolome de Albornoz of the University of Mexico writes against the enslavement and sale of Africans.

1591—Fall of the Empire of Songhai.

1598—Isabel de Olvera, a free mulatta, accompanies the Juan Guerra de Resa Expedition, which colonizes what is now New Mexico.

Timeline: 1601–1700

1602—By Spanish law, mulattoes (people of combined African and European ethnicity), convicts, and "idle" Africans may be shipped to Latin America and forced to work in the mines there.

1607—Jamestown is founded in Virginia.

1609—Fugitive slaves in Mexico, led by Yanga, sign a truce with Spanish colonial authorities and obtain their freedom and a town of their own.

1617—The town of San Lorenzo de los Negros receives a charter from Spanish colonial officials in Mexico and becomes the first officially recognized free settlement for blacks in the New World.

1619—Approximately 20 blacks from a Dutch slaver are purchased as indentured workers for the English settlement of Jamestown. These are the first Africans in the English North American colonies.

1620—The Pilgrims reach New England.

1624—The first African-American child born free in the English colonies, William Tucker, is baptized in Virginia.

1626—The first enslaved Africans arrive in the Dutch Colony of New Amsterdam (now New York City).

1629—The first enslaved Africans arrive in what is now Connecticut.

1634—Slavery is introduced in Maryland.

1638—France's North American colonies open to trade in enslaved Africans.

1641—Massachusetts explicitly permits slavery of Indians, whites, and Negroes in its "Body of Liberties."

1641—Mathias De Sousa, an African indentured servant who came from England with Lord Baltimore, is elected to Maryland's General Assembly.

1642—Virginia passes a fugitive slave law. Offenders helping runaway slaves are fined in pounds of tobacco. An enslaved person is to be branded with a large "R" after a second escape attempt.

When a French privateer brings to New Netherlands some Africans taken from a Spanish ship, they are sold as slaves because of their race, despite their claims to be free.

1643—The New England Confederation reaches an agreement that makes the signature of a magistrate sufficient evidence to re-enslave a suspected fugitive slave.

1645—Merchant ships from Barbados arrive in Boston where they trade their cargoes of enslaved Africans for sugar and tobacco. The profitability of this exchange encourages the slave trade in New England.

c. 1645—Dutch colonists transfer some of their landholdings in New Amsterdam to their former enslaved Africans as compensation for their support in battles with Native Americans. A condition of the land transfer, however, is the guarantee of a specified amount of food from those lands to their former owners.

1646—New Spain's (Colonial Mexico) population includes 35,089 blacks and 116,529 mulattoes.

1650—Connecticut legalizes slavery. Rhode Island by this date has large plantations worked by enslaved Africans.

The Dutch West India Company introduces new rules concerning slavery in New Netherlands. After gaining freedom, former slaves, for example, are required to give fixed amounts of their crops to the company. After the English capture of the colony, greater restrictions are imposed on free blacks and enslaved people.

1651—Anthony Johnson, a free African American, imports several enslaved Africans and is given a grant of land on Virginia's Puwgoteague River. Other free African Americans follow this pattern.

1652—Massachusetts enacts a law requiring all African-American and Native American servants to undergo military training so as to be able to help defend the colony.

1655—Anthony Johnson successfully sues for the return of his slave John Casor, whom the court had earlier treated as an indentured servant.

1656—Fearing the potential for slave uprisings, Massachusetts reverses its 1652 statute and prohibits blacks from arming or training as militia. New Hampshire and New York soon follow.

1660—A Connecticut law prohibits African Americans from serving in the militia.

1662—Virginia reverses the presumption of English law that the child follows the status of his father and enacts a law that makes the free or enslaved status of children dependent on the status of the mother.

1663—Black and white indentured servants plan a rebellion in Gloucester County, Virginia. Their plans are discovered and the leaders are executed.

Maryland slave laws rule that all Africans arriving in the colony are presumed to be slaves. Free European American women who marry enslaved men lose their freedom. Children of European American women and enslaved men are enslaved. Other North American colonies develop similar laws.

In South Carolina every new white settler is granted twenty acres for each black male slave and ten acres for each black female slave he or she brings into the colony.

A planned revolt of enslaved Africans is uncovered in Virginia.

1664—In Virginia, the enslaved African's status is clearly differentiated from the indentured servant's when colonial laws decree that enslavement is for life and is transferred to the children through the mother. Black and "slave" become synonymous, and enslaved Africans are subject to harsher and more brutal control than other laborers.

Maryland establishes slavery for life for persons of African ancestry.

New York and New Jersey also recognize the legality of slavery.

1667—England enacts strict laws regarding enslaved Africans in its colonies. An enslaved African is forbidden to leave the plantation without a pass, and never on Sunday. An enslaved African may not possess weapons or signaling mechanisms such as horns or whistles. Punishment for an owner who kills an enslaved African is a 15-pound fine.

Virginia declares that baptism does not free a slave from bondage, thereby abandoning the Christian tradition of not enslaving other Christians.

1670—A law is enacted in Virginia that all non-Christians who arrive by ship are to be enslaved.

A French royal decree brings French shippers into the slave trade, with the rationale that the labor of enslaved Africans helps the growth of France's island colonies.

The Massachusetts legislature passes a law that enables its citizens to sell the children of enslaved Africans into bondage, thus separating them from their parents.

1671—A Maryland law states that the conversion of enslaved African Americans to Christianity does not affect their status as enslaved people.

1672—King Charles II of England charters the Royal African Company, which dominates the slave trade to North America for the next half-century.

1673—The Massachusetts legislature passes a law that forbids European Americans from engaging in any trade or commerce with an African American.

1675—An estimated 100,000 Africans are enslaved in the West Indies and another 5,000 are in British North America.

1676—Nathaniel Bacon leads an unsuccessful rebellion of whites and blacks against the English colonial government in Virginia.

1681—Maryland laws mandate that children of European servant women and African men are free.

1682—A new slave code in Virginia prohibits weapons for slaves, requires passes beyond the limits of the plantation, and forbids self-defense by any African American against any European American.

1685—New York law forbids enslaved Africans and Native Americans from having meetings or carrying firearms.

1688—Quakers in Germantown, Pennsylvania, denounce slavery in the first recorded formal protest in North America against the enslavement of Africans.

1690—By this year, all English colonies in America have enslaved Africans.

Enslaved Africans and Native Americans in Massachusetts plan a rebellion.

1692—The Virginia House of Burgesses enacts the Runaway Slave Law, making it legal to kill a runaway in the course of apprehension.

1693—All fugitive Africans who have escaped slavery in the British colonies and fled to Florida are granted their freedom by the Spanish monarchy.

1694—The introduction of rice into the Carolina colony, ironically from West Africa, increases the need for labor for emerging plantations. This adds another factor to the economic justification and rationalization for expanding the slave trade.

1696—American Quakers, at their annual meeting, warn members against holding Africans in slavery. Violators who continue to keep slaves are threatened with expulsion.

1700—A census reports more than 27,000 enslaved people, mostly Africans, in the English colonies in North America. The vast majority of these bondspeople live in the southern colonies.

Boston slave traders are involved in selling enslaved Africans in New England colonies and Virginia.

Massachusetts Chief Justice Samuel Sewall publishes *The Selling of Joseph,* a book that advances both the economic and moral reasons for the abolition of the trade in enslaved Africans.

Timeline: 1701–1800

1704—French colonist Elias Neau opens a school for enslaved African Americans in New York City.

1708—Africans in South Carolina outnumber Europeans, making it the first English colony with a black majority.

1711—Great Britain's Queen Anne overrules a Pennsylvania colonial law prohibiting slavery.

1712—The New York City slave revolt begins on April 6. Nine whites are killed and an unknown number of blacks die in the uprising. Colonial authorities execute 21 slaves and six commit suicide.

1713—England secures the exclusive right to transport slaves to the Spanish colonies in America.

1721—South Carolina limits the vote to free white Christian men.

1724—Louisiana's *Code Noir* is enacted in New Orleans to regulate black slavery and banish Jews from the colony.

Boston imposes a curfew on nonwhites.

1727—Enslaved Africans and Native Americans revolt in Middlesex and Gloucester counties in Virginia.

1733—Spain promises freedom in Spanish Florida to slaves who escape from the English colonies.

1735—South Carolina passes laws requiring enslaved people to wear clothing identifying them as slaves. Freed slaves are required to leave the colony within six months or risk re-enslavement.

1737—An indentured black servant petitions a Massachusetts Court and wins his freedom after the death of his master.

1739—The first major South Carolina slave revolt takes place in Stono on September 9. A score of whites and more than twice as many black slaves are killed as the armed slaves try to flee to Florida.

Nineteen white citizens of Darien, Georgia, petition the colonial governor to continue the ban on the importation of Africans into the colony, calling African enslavement "shocking to human nature." This is the first anti-slavery protest in the southern colonies. Ten years later, however, Georgia authorities repeal the ban.

1741—During the New York Slave Conspiracy Trials, New York City officials execute 34 people for planning to burn down the town. Thirteen African-American men are burned at the stake and another 17 black men, two white men, and two white women are hanged. Seventy blacks and seven whites are permanently expelled from the city.

South Carolina's colonial legislature enacts a law banning the teaching of enslaved people to read and write.

1742—New Spain's (Colonial Mexico) population includes 20,131 blacks and 266,196 mulattoes.

1746—Lucy Terry, a slave, composes "Bars Fight," the first known poem by an African American. A description of an Indian raid on Terry's hometown in Massachusetts, the poem will be passed down orally and published in 1855.

1752—Twenty-one-year-old Benjamin Banneker constructs one of the first clocks in Colonial America, the first of a long line of inventions and innovations until his death in 1806.

1758—The African Baptist or "Bluestone" Church is founded on the William Byrd plantation near the Bluestone River, in Mecklenburg, Virginia, becoming the first known black church in North America.

A school for free black children is opened in Philadelphia.

1760—Jupiter Hammon publishes a book of poetry. This is believed to be the first volume written and published by an African American.

1762—Virginia restricts voting rights to white men.

1770—Crispus Attucks, an escaped slave, becomes the first Colonial resident to die for American independence when he is killed by the British in the Boston Massacre.

1772—On June 22, Lord Chief Mansfield rules in the James Somerset case that an enslaved person brought to England becomes free and cannot be returned to slavery, laying the legal basis for the freeing of England's 15,000 slaves.

1773—Phillis Wheatley publishes a book of poetry.

The Silver Bluff Baptist Church, the oldest continuously operating black church, is founded in Silver Bluff, South Carolina, near Savannah, Georgia.

1774—A group of blacks petition the Massachusetts General Court (legislature), insisting they too have a natural right to their freedom.

1775–1781—The American War of Independence. Approximately 450,000 enslaved Africans comprise 20 percent of the population of the colonies at the time of the Declaration of Independence.

1775—African Americans participate on the Patriot side in the earliest battles of the Revolution—Concord, Lexington, and Bunker Hill.

General George Washington reverses his earlier policy of rejecting the services of slaves and free blacks in the army. Five thousand African Americans serve during the Revolutionary War, including two predominantly black units in Massachusetts, one in Connecticut, and one in Rhode Island.

The first Abolition Society meeting in North America is held in Philadelphia; Benjamin Franklin is elected president of the Society.

On November 7, Lord Dunmore, British Governor of Virginia, declares all slaves free who come to the defense of the British Crown against the Patriot forces. Dunmore eventually organizes the first regiment of black soldiers to fight under the British flag.

1776—A passage authored by Thomas Jefferson condemning the slave trade is removed from the Declaration of Independence due to pressure from the southern colonies.

Approximately 100,000 enslaved people flee their masters during the Revolution.

1777—Vermont abolishes slavery.

1778—Boston businessman Paul Cuffe and his brother, John, refuse to pay taxes, claiming as blacks they are not allowed to vote and they suffer taxation without representation.

1780—Massachusetts abolishes slavery and grants African-American men the right to vote.

The Free African Union Society is created in Newport, Rhode Island. It is the first cultural organization established by blacks in North America.

Pennsylvania adopts the first gradual emancipation law. All children of enslaved people born after November 1, 1780, will be free on their 28th birthday.

1781–1783—Twenty-thousand black loyalists depart with British Troops from the newly independent United States. Approximately 5,000 African Americans served with Patriot forces. Three times that many served with the British although not all of them leave the new nation.

1781—Los Angeles is founded by 54 settlers, including 26 of African ancestry.

1784—Connecticut and Rhode Island adopt gradual emancipation laws.

Congress rejects Thomas Jefferson's proposal to exclude slavery from all western territories after 1800.

1785—New York frees all slaves who served in the Revolutionary Army.

1787—Congress enacts the Northwest Ordinance, which establishes formal procedures for transforming territories into states. It provides for the eventual establishment of three to five states in the area north of the Ohio River, to be considered equal with the original 13. The Ordinance includes a Bill of Rights that guarantees freedom of religion, the right to trial by jury, public education, and a ban on slavery in the region.

The U.S. Constitution is drafted. It provides for the continuation of the slave trade for another 20 years and requires states to aid slaveholders in the recovery of fugitive slaves. It also stipulates that a slave counts as three-fifths of a man for purposes of determining representation in the House of Representatives.

Free blacks in New York City found the African Free School, where future leaders Henry Highland Garnet and Alexander Crummell are educated.

Richard Allen and Absalom Jones form the Free African Society in Philadelphia.

1788—In Massachusetts, following an incident in which free blacks were kidnapped and transported to the island of Martinique, the Massachusetts legislature declares the slave trade illegal and provides monetary damages to victims of kidnappings.

1789—The French Revolution begins.

1790—First Census of the United States
　　U.S. Population: 3,929,214
　　Black Population: 757,208 (19.3%), including 59,557 free African Americans.

Free African Americans in Charleston form the Brown Fellowship Society.

1791—The Haitian Revolution begins.

1793—The United States Congress enacts the first Fugitive Slave Law. Providing assistance to fugitive slaves is now a criminal offense.

Eli Whitney patents the cotton gin on March 13, which begins the slave-based "cotton economy" of the South.

1794—The French government abolishes slavery. The law is repealed by Napoleon in 1802.

Mother Bethel AME Church is established in Philadelphia.

New York adopts a gradual emancipation law.

1793—New Spain's (Colonial Mexico) population includes 6,100 blacks and 369,790 mulattoes.

1795—Bowdoin College is founded in Maine. It later becomes a center for abolitionist activity; Gen. Oliver O. Howard (Howard University) graduated from the college; Harriet Beecher Stowe taught there and began to write *Uncle Tom's Cabin* while there (in 1850).

1796—On August 23, The African Methodist Episcopal (AME) Church is organized in Philadelphia.

1800—Census of 1800
    U.S. Population: 5,308,483
    Black Population: 1,002,037 (18.9%), including 108,435 free African Americans.

Gabriel Prosser attempts a slave rebellion in Virginia.

The United States Congress rejects 85 to 1 an anti-slavery petition offered by free Philadelphia African Americans.

Timeline: 1801–1900

1802—The Ohio Constitution outlaws slavery. It also prohibits free blacks from voting. The Ohio Legislature passes the first "Black Laws," which place other restrictions on free African Americans living in the state.

James Callender claims that Thomas Jefferson has "for many years past kept, as his concubine, one of his own slaves," Sally

Hemings. His charge is published in the Richmond *Recorder,* and the story is soon picked up by the Federalist press around the country.

1803—On April 30, Louisiana is purchased from the French. The new territory nearly doubles the size of the United States.

1804—On January 1, Haiti becomes an independent nation. It is the second independent nation in the Western Hemisphere (after the United States).

1804–1806—The Lewis and Clark Expedition explores newly purchased Louisiana and the Pacific Northwest. An African American, York, is prominent in the expedition.

1807—Great Britain abolishes the importation of enslaved Africans into its colonial possessions.

New Jersey disfranchises black voters.

1808—The United States government abolishes the importation of enslaved Africans; however, the ban is widely ignored. Between 1808 and 1860, approximately 250,000 blacks are illegally imported into the United States. Slave trading within the states (the domestic trade) continues until the end of the Civil War.

1809—New York recognizes marriage within the African-American community.

Abyssinian Baptist Church, destined to become by the 1930s the largest church in the United States, is founded in New York City.

1810—Census of 1810
    U.S. Population: 7,239,881
    Black Population: 1,377,808 (19%), including 186,446 free African Americans.

The U.S. Congress prohibits African Americans from carrying mail for the U.S. Postal Service.

1811—Andry's Rebellion on January 8–11. A slave insurrection led by Charles Deslondes begins on the Louisiana plantation of Manual Andry.

1812—Previously independent African-American schools become part of the Boston public school system.

Two African-American regiments are formed in New York to fight in the War of 1812.

1814—Six hundred African-American troops are among the U.S. Army of 3,000 led by General Andrew Jackson, which defeats British forces at the Battle of New Orleans.

1815—Richard Allen officially creates the African Methodist Episcopal Church, the first wholly African-American church denomination in the United States.

Abolitionist Levi Coffin establishes the Underground Railroad.

1816—The American Colonization Society is founded by Bushrod Washington (the nephew of George Washington) and other prominent white Americans who believe enslaved African Americans should be freed and settled in Africa.

1817–1818—Escaped slaves from Georgia, South Carolina, and Alabama join the military campaign of the Florida Seminoles to keep their homelands.

1818—Connecticut disfranchises black voters.

1819—The Canadian government refuses to cooperate with the American government in the apprehension of fugitive slaves living in Canada.

1820—Census of 1820
    U.S. Population: 9,638,452
    Black Population: 1,771,656 (18.4%), including 233,504 free African Americans.

The Compromise of 1820 allows Missouri into the Union as a slave state and Maine as a free state. It also sets the boundary between slave and free territory in the West at the 36th parallel.

Rev. Daniel Coker of Baltimore leads 86 African Americans who become the first black settlers to Liberia.

1821—New York maintains property qualifications for African-American male voters while abolishing the same for white male voters. Missouri disfranchises free black male voters.

1822—Denmark Vesey is arrested for planning a slave rebellion in South Carolina.

Rhode Island disfranchises black voters.

1824—Mexico outlaws slavery. This act creates the incentive for Anglo Texans to fight for independence.

A white mob destroys the African-American community of Providence, Rhode Island.

1826—On August 23, Edward Jones receives a degree from Amherst College in Massachusetts, becoming the first African-American college graduate.

1827—*Freedom's Journal* begins publication on March 16 in New York City as the first African-American-owned newspaper in the United States. The editors are John Russwurm and Samuel Cornish.

Slavery is officially abolished in New York.

1829—More than half of Cincinnati's African-American residents are driven out of the city by white mob violence. The Cincinnati riots usher in a more-than-century-long period of white violence against northern black urban communities.

David Walker of Boston publishes *An Appeal to the Colored Citizens of the World,* which calls for a slave uprising in the South.

1830—Census of 1830
    U.S. Population: 12,866,020
    Black Population: 2,328,842 (18.1%), including 319,599 free African Americans.

African-American delegates from New York, Pennsylvania, Maryland, Delaware, and Virginia meet in Philadelphia in the first of a series of National Negro Conventions to devise ways to challenge slavery in the South and racial discrimination in the North.

The American Society of Free People of Colour is organized in Philadelphia.

1831—North Carolina enacts a statute that bans teaching slaves to read and write.

Nat Turner leads a slave rebellion in Southampton, Virginia, killing at least 57 whites.

Alabama makes it illegal for enslaved or free blacks to preach.

William Lloyd Garrison of Boston founds *The Liberator*, the first abolitionist newspaper in the United States.

1832—Oberlin College is founded in Ohio. It admits African-American men, black women, and white women. By 1860 one-third of its students are black.

The Female Anti-Slavery Society, the first African-American women's abolitionist society, is founded in Salem, Massachusetts.

1833—The American Anti-Slavery Society is established in Philadelphia, Pennsylvania.

The British Parliament abolishes slavery in the entire British Empire.

1834—African Free Schools are incorporated into the New York Public School system.

Henry Blair is the first African American to receive a patent from the U.S. government. He develops a mechanical corn planter.

South Carolina bans the teaching of blacks, enslaved or free, within its borders.

1835—Texas declares its independence from Mexico. In its Constitution as an independent nation, Texas recognizes slavery and makes it difficult for free blacks to remain there.

1836–1844—The "Gag Rule" prohibits Congress from considering petitions regarding slavery.

1836—John B. Russwurm is appointed Governor of the Cape Palmas district of Liberia by the American Colonization Society.

1837—The Institute for Colored Youth is founded in Southeastern Pennsylvania. It later becomes Cheyney University.

Dr. James McCune Smith of New York City graduates from the Medical School of the University of Glasgow and becomes the first African American to hold a medical degree.

1838—Pennsylvania disfranchises black voters.

1839—On August 29, American vessels tow the Spanish ship the *Amistad* and its 53 slaves into New London, Connecticut. Their fate is decided by the United States Supreme Court in *United States v. The Amistad* on March 9, 1841, when the Court rules them free and they return to Africa.

1840—Census of 1840
U.S. Population: 17,069,453
Black Population: 2,873,648 (16.1%), including 386,293 free African Americans.

1841—*The Christian Recorder,* the publication of the African Methodist Episcopal Church, appears for the first time in Philadelphia. The *Recorder* is the oldest continuously published African-American periodical in the United States.

1842—Frederick Douglass leads a successful campaign against Rhode Island's proposed Dorr Constitution, which continues the prohibition on black voting rights.

The Virginia Legislature votes against abolishing slavery.

1843—Rev. Henry Highland Garnet delivers his controversial "Address to the Slaves" at the National Negro Convention meeting in Buffalo, New York, which calls for a servile insurrection.

Sojourner Truth and William Wells Brown begin their campaigns against slavery.

1844—On June 25, the Legislative Committee of the Provisional Government of Oregon enacts the first of a series of black exclusion laws.

1845—Texas is annexed to the United States.

Frederick Douglass publishes his autobiography, *The Life and Times of Frederick Douglass.*

1846–1848—War with Mexico.

1847—Frederick Douglass, Martin Delany, and William C. Nell begin publication of *The North Star* in Rochester, New York.

Missouri bans the education of free blacks.

Missouri abolitionists file a lawsuit on behalf of Dred Scott to gain his freedom. The case is eventually decided by the U.S. Supreme Court a decade later.

1848—On February 2 in the Treaty of Guadalupe Hidalgo, Mexico cedes California, Arizona, New Mexico, Nevada, and Utah and gives up claim to Texas at the conclusion of war in exchange for $20 million.

In February Karl Marx publishes *The Communist Manifesto* in London.

On July 19–20, Frederick Douglass is among the handful of men who attend the first Women's Rights Convention at Seneca Falls, New York.

1849—The California Gold Rush begins. Eventually four-thousand African Americans will migrate to California during this period.

Harriett Tubman escapes from slavery and begins her efforts to rescue enslaved people.

On December 4, Benjamin Roberts files a school desegregation lawsuit on behalf of his daughter, Sarah, who is denied admission to a Boston school. The lawsuit is unsuccessful.

1850—Census of 1850
U.S. Population: 23,191,876
Black Population: 3,638,808 (15.7%), including 433,807 free African Americans.

The Compromise of 1850 revisits the issue of slavery. California enters the Union as a free state, but the territories of New Mexico and Utah are allowed to decide whether they will enter the Union as slave or free states. The 1850 Compromise also allows passage of a much stricter Fugitive Slave Law.

On August 27, Lucy Stanton of Cleveland completes the course requirements for Oberlin Collegiate Institute (now Oberlin College) and becomes the first African-American woman to graduate from an American college or university.

1851—Sojourner Truth delivers her famous "Ain't I a Woman?" speech at the Women's Rights Convention, Akron, Ohio, on May 29.

1852—Harriet Beecher Stowe publishes her novel, *Uncle Tom's Cabin*, which becomes a best-selling book and a major influence on the anti-slavery movement.

Martin R. Delany publishes *The Condition, Elevation, Emigration, and Destiny of the Colored People of the United States.*

The Jackson Street Hospital in Augusta, Georgia, is established as the first medical facility solely for the care of African-American patients.

1853—Elizabeth Taylor Greenfield (the "Black Swan") debuts at the Metropolitan Opera in New York City and performs before Queen Victoria at Buckingham Palace a year later.

William Wells Brown becomes the first African-American novelist when he publishes *Clotel, or the President's Daughter.*

1854—On May 24, Virginia fugitive slave Anthony Burns is captured in Boston and returned to slavery under the provisions of the Fugitive Slave Act. Fifty-thousand Boston residents watch his transport through the streets of the city in shackles. A Boston church raises $1,500 to purchase his freedom, and Burns returns to the city in 1855, a free man.

On May 30, the Kansas-Nebraska Act is passed by Congress. The Act repeals the Missouri Compromise and permits the admission of Kansas and Nebraska Territories to the Union after their populations decide on slavery.

The Republican Party is formed in the summer in opposition to the extension of slavery into the western territories.

"Bleeding Kansas" is an outgrowth of the controversy over the Kansas-Nebraska Act. Between 1854 and 1858 armed groups of pro- and anti-slavery factions, often funded and sponsored by organizations in the North and South, compete for control of Kansas Territory, initiating waves of violence that killed 55 people. Bleeding Kansas was seen as a preview of the U.S. Civil War.

On October 13, Ashmun Institute, the first institution of higher learning for young black men, is founded by John Miller Dickey and his wife, Sarah Emlen Cresson. In 1866 it is renamed Lincoln University (PA) after President Abraham Lincoln.

James A. Healy is ordained in France as the first black Jesuit priest. He becomes Bishop of Portland, Maine, in 1875, a diocese that includes all of Maine and New Hampshire, and holds that post for 25 years.

1855—The Massachusetts Legislature outlaws racially segregated schools.

William C. Nell of Boston publishes *The Colored Patriots of the American Revolution*, considered the first history of African Americans.

In November, John Mercer Langston is elected town clerk of Brownhelm Township, Ohio, becoming the first black elected official in the nation.

1856—Wilberforce University becomes the first school of higher learning owned and operated by African Americans. It is founded by the African Methodist Episcopal Church. Bishop Daniel A. Payne becomes the institution's first president.

1857—On March 6, The *Dred Scott* decision is handed down by the U.S. Supreme Court.

1858—Arkansas enslaves free blacks who refuse to leave the state.

1859—On October 16, John Brown leads twenty men, including five African Americans, in an unsuccessful attempt to seize the Federal Armory at Harper's Ferry, Virginia, to inspire a servile insurrection.

Harriett Wilson of Milford, New Hampshire, publishes *Our Nig; or Sketches from the Life of a Free Black,* the first novel by an African-American woman.

1860—Census of 1860
 U.S. Population: 31,443,321
 Black Population: 4,441,830 (14.1%), including 488,070 free African Americans.

On November 6, Abraham Lincoln is elected president.

On December 20, South Carolina secedes from the Union.

1861—By February, Mississippi, Florida, Alabama, Georgia, Louisiana, and Texas secede. They form the Confederate States of America on March 4. After the firing on Fort Sumter near Charleston, South Carolina, on April 12, Virginia, Arkansas, Tennessee, and North Carolina secede.

1861–1865—The Civil War. Approximately 200,000 blacks (most are newly escaped/freed slaves) serve in Union armed forces, and over 20,000 are killed in combat.

1861—Congress passes the First Confiscation Act, which prevents Confederate slave owners from re-enslaving runaways.

1862—The Port Royal (South Carolina) Reconstruction Experiment begins in March.

On April 16, Congress abolishes slavery in the District of Columbia.

In May the coastal pilot Robert Smalls escapes Charleston, South Carolina, with *The Planter*, a Confederate vessel and sixteen enslaved people.

Congress permits the enlistment of African-American soldiers in the U.S. Army on July 17.

With the southern states absent from Congress, the body recognizes Haiti and Liberia, marking the first time diplomatic relations are established with predominately black nations.

1863—Abraham Lincoln's Emancipation Proclamation takes effect on January 1, legally freeing slaves in areas of the South still in rebellion against the United States.

The New York City draft riots erupt on July 13 and continue for four days, during which at least 100 of the city's residents are killed. This remains the highest death toll in any urban conflict in the 19th or 20th centuries.

On July 18, the Fifty-Fourth Massachusetts Volunteers, the first officially recognized all-black military unit in the Union army, assaults Fort Wagner in Charleston, South Carolina, in an unsuccessful effort to take the fortification. Sergeant William H. Carney becomes the first African American to receive the Congressional Medal of Honor for bravery under fire.

1864—The Fort Pillow Massacre takes place in West Tennessee on April 12. Approximately 300 of the 585 soldiers of the Union garrison at Fort Pillow are killed, including many after the Union forces surrender. Only 14 Confederate soldiers die in the battle.

In June, Dr. Rebecca Lee Crumpler of Boston is the first African-American woman to earn a medical degree when she graduates from the New England Female Medical College in Boston.

On June 15, Congress passes a bill authorizing equal pay, equipment, arms, and healthcare for African-American Union troops.

On October 4, the New Orleans *Tribune* begins publication. The *Tribune* is the first daily newspaper produced by African Americans.

1865—On February 1, 1865, Abraham Lincoln signs the 13th Amendment to the U.S. Constitution, outlawing slavery throughout the United States.

Upon the order of President Abraham Lincoln, Martin Robinson Delany is the first African American commissioned as a field officer. He holds the rank of major in the regular infantry.

On March 3, Congress establishes the Freedmen's Bureau to provide healthcare, education, and technical assistance to emancipated slaves. Congress also charters the Freedman's Bank to promote savings and thrift among the ex-slaves.

Confederate General Robert E. Lee surrenders to Union General Ulysses S. Grant on April 9 at Appomattox Court House, Virginia, effectively ending the Civil War.

On April 15, President Abraham Lincoln is assassinated by John Wilkes Booth in Washington, DC.

On June 19, enslaved African Americans in Texas finally receive news of their emancipation. From that point they commemorate that day as "Juneteenth."

Between September and November, a number of ex-Confederate states pass so-called "Black Codes."

The Ku Klux Klan is formed on December 24th in Pulaski, Tennessee, by six educated, middle-class former Confederate veterans.

Twenty-thousand African-American troops are among the 32,000 U.S. soldiers sent to the Rio Grande as a show of force against Emperor Maximilian's French troops occupying Mexico. Some discharged black soldiers join the forces of Mexican resistance leader Benito Juarez.

1866—Fisk University is founded in Nashville, Tennessee, on January 9.

On April 9, Congress overrides President Andrew Johnson's veto to enact the Civil Rights Act of 1866. The act confers citizenship upon black Americans and guarantees equal rights with whites.

On May 1–3, white civilians and police in Memphis, Tennessee, kill forty-six African Americans and injure many more, burning ninety houses, twelve schools, and four churches in what will be known as the Memphis Massacre.

On June 13, Congress approves the Fourteenth Amendment to the Constitution, guaranteeing due process and equal protection under the law to all citizens. The amendment also grants citizenship to African Americans.

Congress authorizes the creation of four all-black regiments in the United States Army. Two cavalry regiments, the 9th and 10th, and two infantry regiments, the 24th and 25th, will become the first and only units in which black soldiers can serve until the Spanish American War. They will be known as Buffalo Soldiers.

Police in New Orleans supporting the Democratic mayor storm a Republican meeting of blacks and whites on July 30th, killing 34 black and three white Republicans. Over 150 people are injured in the attack.

In November Mifflin W. Gibbs is elected to the Victoria, British Columbia, City Council. He becomes the second African American (after John Mercer Langston) elected to public office in North America.

1867—On January 8, overriding President Andrew Johnson's veto, Congress grants the black citizens of the District of Columbia the right to vote. Two days later it passes the Territorial Suffrage Act, which allows African Americans in the western territories to vote.

Morehouse College is founded in Atlanta on February 14.

The Reconstruction Acts are passed by Congress on March 2. Congress divides ten of the eleven ex-Confederate states into military districts. These acts also reorganize post-war southern governments, disfranchising former high-ranking Confederates and enfranchising former slaves in the South.

On March 2, Howard University is chartered by Congress in Washington, DC. The institution is named after General Oliver O. Howard who heads the Freedman's Bureau.

1868—On July 21, the Fourteenth Amendment to the Constitution is ratified, granting citizenship to any person born or naturalized in the United States.

Opelousas, Louisiana, is the site of the Opelousas Massacre on September 28, in which an estimated 200 to 300 black Americans are killed by whites opposed to Reconstruction and African-American voting.

On November 3, Civil War general Ulysses S. Grant (Republican) is elected president.

On November 3, John Willis Menard is elected to Congress from Louisiana's Second Congressional District. Menard is the first African American elected to Congress. However, neither he nor his opponent will be seated due to disputed election results.

Howard University Medical School opens on November 9.

1869—On February 26, Congress sends the Fifteenth Amendment to the Constitution to the states for approval. The amendment guarantees African-American males the right to vote.

On April 6, Ebenezer Don Carlos Bassett is appointed minister to Haiti. He is the first black American diplomat and presidential appointee.

Mary Ann Shadd tries to register to vote in Washington, DC. When she is turned away, she petitions Congress to extend the vote to women.

Isaac Myers organizes the Colored National Labor Union in Baltimore.

1870—Census of 1870
    U.S. Population: 39,818,449
    Black Population: 4,880,009 (12.7%)

Hiram R. Revels (Republican) of Mississippi takes his seat in the U.S. Senate on February 25. He is the first black United States senator, though he serves only one year, completing the unexpired term of Jefferson Davis.

The Fifteenth Amendment to the Constitution is ratified on March 30.

In June Richard T. Greener becomes the first African American to graduate from Harvard University.

In December Robert H. Wood is elected mayor of Natchez, Mississippi. He is one of the earliest African-American mayors in the nation.

1871—In February Congress passes the Civil Rights Act of 1871, popularly known as the Ku Klux Klan Act.

On October 6, Fisk University's Jubilee Singers begin their first national tour. The Jubilee Singers become world-famous singers of black spirituals, performing before the Queen of England and the Emperor of Japan. The money they earn finances the construction of Jubilee Hall on the Fisk University campus.

1872—Charlotte Ray of Washington, DC, becomes the first African-American woman to practice law.

Lt. Governor Pinckney Benton Stewart Pinchback of Louisiana serves as governor of the state for one month, from December 1872 to January 1873. He is the first African American to hold that position.

1873—The 43rd Congress has seven black members.

On April 14, the U.S Supreme Court in the *Slaughterhouse* cases rules that the "due process" clause of the 14th Amendment protects national, not state, citizenship.

Bishop Patrick Healy serves as President of Georgetown University from 1873 to 1881. He is the first African American to preside over a predominately white university.

1874—The Freedman's Bank closes after African-American depositors and investors lose more than one million dollars.

1875—Federal troops are sent to Vicksburg, Mississippi, in January to protect African Americans attempting to vote and to allow the safe return of the African-American sheriff who had been forced to flee the city.

Congress enacts the Civil Rights Act of 1875 on March 1, guaranteeing equal rights to black Americans in public accommodations and jury duty.

Blanche Kelso Bruce (Republican) of Mississippi becomes the first African American to serve a full six-year term as senator when he takes his seat in the United States Senate on March 3.

The 44th Congress has eight black members.

On February 23rd the first southern "Jim Crow" laws are enacted in Tennessee. Similar statutes had existed in the North before the Civil War.

1876—Lewis H. Latimer assists Alexander Graham Bell in obtaining a patent for the telephone on February 14.

In May, Edward Alexander Bouchet receives a Ph.D. degree from Yale University. He is the first African American to receive a Ph.D. from an American university and only the sixth American to earn a Ph.D. in physics. Bouchet is also believed to be the first African American elected to Phi Beta Kappa.

Race riots and other forms of terrorism against black voters in South Carolina over the summer prompt President Grant to send federal troops to restore order.

On October 13, Meharry Medical College is founded by the Freedman's Aid Society of the Methodist Church.

Harriett Purvis is elected the first black president of the American Woman Suffrage Association.

The presidential election of 1876, pitting Samuel Tilden (Democrat) against Rutherford B. Hayes (Republican), is inconclusive when the votes in the Electoral College are disputed.

1877—The Compromise of 1877 (also known as the Wormley House Compromise because the meeting takes place in a black-owned hotel in Washington, DC) is an arrangement worked out in January of that year, which effectively ends Reconstruction. Although Democratic presidential candidate Samuel Tilden won the popular vote, southern Democratic leaders agree to support Rutherford Hayes's efforts to obtain the disputed electoral votes of Florida, Louisiana, and South Carolina in exchange for the withdrawal of the last federal troops from the South and the end of federal efforts to protect the civil rights of African Americans.

The 45th Congress has three black members.

On June 15, Henry O. Flipper becomes the first African American to graduate from West Point.

In July, 30 African-American settlers from Kentucky establish the town of Nicodemus in western Kansas. This is the first of hundreds of all or mostly black towns created in the West.

Frederick Douglass becomes U.S. Marshal for the District of Columbia.

1879–1880—Approximately six-thousand African Americans leave Louisiana and Mississippi counties along the Mississippi River for Kansas in what will be known as the Exodus.

1879—Mary Eliza Mahoney becomes the first African-American professional nurse, graduating from the New England Hospital for Women and Children in Boston.

The Liberia Exodus Joint Stock Company sends the first post–Civil War African-American emigrants to West Africa on the ship *Azor.*

1880—Census of 1880
    U.S. Population: 50,155,783
    Black Population: 6,580,793 (13.1%)

On May 14, Sgt. George Jordan of the Ninth Cavalry, commanding a detachment of Buffalo Soldiers, leads a successful defense of Tularosa, New Mexico Territory, against Apache Indians.

1881—In January the Tennessee State Legislature votes to segregate railroad passenger cars. Tennessee's action is followed by Florida (1887), Mississippi (1888), Texas (1889), Louisiana (1890), Alabama, Kentucky, Arkansas, and Georgia (1891), South Carolina (1898), North Carolina (1899), Virginia (1900), Maryland (1904), and Oklahoma (1907).

Spelman College, the first college for black women in the United States, is founded on April 11 by Sophia B. Packard and Harriet E. Giles.

On the Fourth of July Booker T. Washington opens Tuskegee Institute in central Alabama.

1883—On January 13 former slaves found the Richmond *Planet* in Richmond, Virginia. Edited between 1884 and 1929 by John Mitchell, Jr., it becomes one of the most successful papers of its era.

The 50th Congress has no black members. Intimidation keeps most black voters from the polls.

On October 16, the U. S. Supreme Court declares invalid the Civil Rights Act of 1875, stating the federal government cannot bar corporations or individuals from discriminating on the basis of race.

On November 3, white conservatives in Danville, Virginia, seize control of the local racially integrated and popularly elected government, killing four African Americans in the process.

1884—Christopher J. Perry establishes the Philadelphia *Tribune*, the longest, continuously operating African-American newspaper in the nation.

1885—On June 25, African-American Samuel David Ferguson is ordained a bishop of the Episcopal Church.

1886—Slavery is abolished in Cuba.

The Knights of Labor reaches its peak membership of 700,000 with approximately 75,000 African-American members.

The American Federation of Labor is organized on December 8. All major unions of the federation excluded black workers.

1887—African-American players are banned from major league baseball.

The National Colored Farmers' Alliance is formed in Houston County, Texas.

1888—On April 11, Edward Park Duplex is elected mayor of Wheatland, California. He is believed to be the first African-American mayor of a predominantly white town in the United States.

Two of America's first black-owned banks, the Savings Bank of the Grand Fountain United Order of the Reformers, in Richmond, Virginia, and Capital Savings Bank of Washington, DC, open their doors.

Slavery is abolished in Brazil.

1889—Florida becomes the first state to use the poll tax to disenfranchise black voters.

Frederick Douglass is appointed Minister to Haiti.

1890—Census of 1890
U.S. Population: 62,947,714
Black Population: 7,488,676 (11.9%)

The Afro-American League is founded on January 25 in Chicago under the leadership of Timothy Thomas Fortune.

On November 1, the Mississippi Legislature approves a new state Constitution that disfranchises virtually all of the state's African-American voters. The Mississippi Plan used literacy and "understanding" tests to prevent African Americans from casting ballots. Similar statutes were adopted by South Carolina (1895), Louisiana (1898), North Carolina (1900), Alabama (1901), Virginia (1901), Georgia (1908), and Oklahoma (1910).

1891—Dr. Daniel Hale Williams founds Provident Hospital in Chicago, the first African-American-owned hospital in the nation.

1892—On July 14 three companies of the 24th Infantry occupy the Coeur d'Alene Mining District in northern Idaho, which has been declared under martial law following a violent strike by silver miners. They remain for four months.

A record 230 people are lynched in the United States this year; 161 are black and 69 white. In the period between 1882 and 1951, Tuskegee Institute compiled nationwide lynching statistics. In that 69-year period, 4,730 people were lynched, including 3,437 blacks and 1,293 whites. Ninety-two women were victims of lynching, 76 were black and 16 were white. Although southern states accounted for 90 percent of the lynchings, every state in the continental United States, with the exception of Massachusetts, Rhode Island, New Hampshire, and Vermont, reported lynching deaths sometime during the 69-year period.

In October activist Ida B. Wells begins her anti-lynching campaign with the publication of *Southern Horrors: Lynch Law in All Its Phases* and a speech in New York City's Lyric Hall.

The National Medical Association is formed in Atlanta by African-American physicians because they are barred from the American Medical Association.

The first intercollegiate football game between African-American colleges takes place between Biddle University (now Johnson C. Smith University) and Livingston College.

1893—Henry Ossawa Tanner paints *The Banjo Lesson,* which is eventually hailed as one of the major works of art of the late 19th century.

Dr. Daniel Hale Williams performs the first successful operation on a human heart. The patient, a victim of a chest stab wound, survives and lives for twenty years after the operation.

1895—White terrorists attack black workers in New Orleans on March 11–12. Six blacks are killed.

In June, W.E.B. Du Bois becomes the first African American to receive a Ph.D. degree from Harvard University.

Booker T. Washington delivers his famous "Atlanta Compromise" address on September 18 at the Atlanta Cotton States Exposition. He says the "Negro problem" would be solved by a policy of gradualism and accommodation.

Three black Baptist organizations—the Foreign Mission Baptist Convention of the United States (1880), the American National Baptist Convention (1886), and the Baptist National Educational Convention (1893)—combined at Friendship Baptist Church in Atlanta to form the National Baptist Convention of America, Inc. The National Baptist Convention is the largest black religious denomination in the United States.

1896—*Plessy v. Ferguson* is decided on May 18 when the U.S. Supreme Court rules that southern segregation laws and practices (Jim Crow) do not conflict with the 13th and 14th Amendments. The Court defends its ruling by articulating the "separate but equal" doctrine.

On July 21 the National Association of Colored Women is formed in Washington, DC. Mary Church Terrell is chosen as its first president.

In September George Washington Carver is appointed director of agricultural research at Tuskegee Institute. His work advances peanut, sweet potato, and soybean farming.

1897—The American Negro Academy is established on March 5 in Washington, DC, to encourage African-American participation in art, literature, and philosophy.

The first Phillis Wheatley Home is founded in Detroit. These homes, established in most cities with large African-American populations, provide temporary accommodations and social services for single African-American women.

1898—In January the Louisiana Legislature introduces the "Grandfather Clause" into the state's constitution. Only males whose fathers or grandfathers were qualified to vote on January 1, 1867, are automatically registered. Others (African Americans) must comply with educational or property requirements.

The Spanish-American War begins on April 21. Sixteen regiments of black volunteers are recruited; four see combat in Cuba and the Philippines. Five African Americans win Congressional Medals of Honor during the war. A number of black officers command troops for the first time.

The National Afro-American Council is founded on September 15 in Washington, DC. The organization elects Bishop Alexander Walters as its first president.

On November 10, in Wilmington, North Carolina, eight black Americans are killed during white rioting as conservative Democrats drive out of power black and white Republican officeholders in the city.

The North Carolina Mutual and Provident Insurance Company of Durham, North Carolina, and the National Benefit Life Insurance Company of Washington, DC, are established.

1899—In May, the 24th Infantry returns to occupy the Coeur d'Alene Mining District in northern Idaho after violence again erupts.

The Afro-American Council designates June 4 as a national day of fasting to protest lynching and massacres.

1900—Census of 1900
U.S. Population: 75,994,575
Black Population: 8,833,994 (11.6%)

In January James Weldon Johnson writes the lyrics and his brother John Rosamond Johnson composes the music for *Lift Every*

Voice and Sing in their hometown of Jacksonville, Florida, in celebration of the birthday of Abraham Lincoln. The song is eventually adopted as the black national anthem.

The United States Pavilion at the Paris Exposition (April 14–November 10) houses an exhibition on black Americans called the *Exposition des Negres d'Amerique.*

The first Pan African Conference, organized by Henry Sylvester Williams, a Trinidad attorney, meets in London in July.

The New Orleans Race Riot (also known as the Robert Charles Riot) erupts on July 23 and lasts four days. Twelve African Americans and seven whites are killed.

On August 23, the National Negro Business League is founded in Boston by Booker T. Washington to promote business enterprise.

In September Nannie Helen Burroughs leads the founding of the Women's Convention of the National Baptist Convention at its meeting in Richmond, Virginia.

This year marks the beginning of significant West Indian immigration to the United States.

Timeline: 1901–2000

1901—The last African-American Congressman elected in the 19th century, George H. White, Republican of North Carolina, leaves office. No African American will serve in Congress for the next 28 years.

On October 11, when Bert Williams and George Walker record their music for the Victor Talking Machine Company, they become the first African-American recording artists.

On October 16, only one month after becoming president, Theodore Roosevelt holds an afternoon meeting at the White House with Booker T. Washington. At the end of the meeting, the president informally invites Washington to remain for dinner, making the Tuskegee educator the first black American to dine at the White House with a president. Roosevelt's casual act generates a national furor.

1902—In May jockey Jimmy Winkfield wins the Kentucky Derby in an era when African-American jockeys dominate the sport.

1903—W.E.B. Du Bois's *The Souls of Black Folk* is published on April 27. In it Du Bois rejects the gradualism of Booker T. Washington, calling for agitation on behalf of African-American rights.

Maggie Lena Walker founds St. Luke's Penny Savings Bank in Richmond, Virginia.

Meta Vaux Warrick, an African-American sculptor, exhibits her work at the Paris Salon, Paris, France.

1904—Educator Mary McLeod Bethune founds a college in Daytona Beach, Florida, that today is known as Bethune-Cookman College.

Sigma Pi Beta (the *Boule*) is founded in Philadelphia by four wealthy African-American college graduates.

Dr. Solomon Carter Fuller, who trains at the Royal Psychiatric Hospital at the University of Munich with Dr. Alois Alzheimer, becomes a widely published pioneer in Alzheimer's disease research. Fuller also becomes the nation's first black psychiatrist.

1905—The Chicago *Defender* is founded by Robert Abbott on May 5.

The Niagara Movement is created on July 11–13, by African-American intellectuals and activists, led by W.E.B. Du Bois and William Monroe Trotter.

Nashville African Americans boycott streetcars to protest racial segregation.

1906—The Azusa Street Revival begins in the former African Methodist Episcopal Church building at 312 Azusa Street, Houston, Texas, in April. The revival, led by black evangelist

William J. Seymour, is considered the beginning of the worldwide Pentecostal Movement.

On August 13 in Brownsville, Texas, approximately a dozen black troops riot against segregation and in the process kill a local citizen. When the identity of the killer cannot be determined, President Theodore Roosevelt discharges three companies of black soldiers on November 6.

A race riot in Atlanta on September 22–24 produces twelve deaths: ten blacks and two whites.

On December 4, seven students at Cornell University form Alpha Phi Alpha Fraternity, the first college fraternity for black men.

1907—Alain Locke of Philadelphia, a Harvard graduate, becomes the first African-American Rhodes Scholar.

The Pittsburgh *Courier* is established by Edwin Harleston, a security guard and an aspiring writer. Three years later attorney Robert Vann takes control of the paper as its editor-publisher.

Madame C.J. Walker of Denver develops and markets her hair-straightening method and creates one of the most successful cosmetics firms in the nation.

1908—On January 15, Alpha Kappa Alpha, the first black sorority, is founded on the campus of Howard University.

John Baxter "Doc" Taylor of the University of Pennsylvania becomes the first African American to win an Olympic Gold Medal. His event is the 4/400-meter medley at the London Games.

On August 14, a two-day race riot breaks out in Springfield, Illinois, the hometown of Abraham Lincoln. Two blacks and four whites are killed. This is the first major riot in a northern city in nearly half a century.

On December 26, Jack Johnson defeats Canadian Tommy Burns in Sydney, Australia, to become the first African-American heavyweight boxing champion of the world.

1909—The National Association for the Advancement of Colored People (NAACP) is formed on February 12 in New York City, partly in response to the Springfield Riot.

On April 6, Admiral Robert E. Peary and African-American Matthew Henson, accompanied by four Eskimos, become the first men known to have reached the North Pole.

On December 4, the New York *Amsterdam News* begins publication.

1910—Census of 1910
    U.S. Population: 93,402,151
    Black Population: 9,827,763 (10.7%)

The National Urban League is founded in New York City on September 29. The League is organized to help African Americans secure employment and to adjust to urban life.

The first issue of *Crisis,* the official publication of the NAACP, appears on November 1. W.E.B. Du Bois is the first editor.

On December 19, the City Council of Baltimore approves an ordinance segregating black and white neighborhoods. This ordinance is followed by similar statutes in Dallas, Texas; Greensboro, North Carolina; Louisville, Kentucky; Norfolk, Virginia; Oklahoma City, Oklahoma; Richmond, Virginia; Roanoke, Virginia; and St. Louis, Missouri.

1911—Kappa Alpha Psi Fraternity is founded at Indiana University on January 5.

Omega Psi Phi Fraternity is founded at Howard University on November 17.

1913—The Jubilee year, the 50th anniversary of the Emancipation Proclamation, is celebrated throughout the nation over the entire year.

Delta Sigma Theta Sorority is founded at Howard University on January 13.

On April 11, the Wilson administration initiates the racial segregation of work places, restrooms, and lunch rooms in all federal offices across the nation.

Bert Williams plays the lead role in *Darktown Jubilee,* making him the first African-American actor to star in a motion picture.

1914—Phi Beta Sigma Fraternity is founded at Howard University on January 9.

The Universal Negro Improvement Association (UNIA) is founded in Kingston, Jamaica, by Marcus and Amy Jacques Garvey.

Cleveland inventor Garrett Morgan patents a gas mask called the Safety Hood and Smoke Protector. The mask, initially used to rescue trapped miners, is eventually adopted by the U.S. Army.

On August 1, World War I begins in Europe.

African-American pilot Eugene J. Bullard volunteers to serve with the French Air Force in World War I. He is the first black pilot to see combat in that conflict.

1915—The Great Migration of African Americans from the South to northern cities begins.

On June 21, the Oklahoma Grandfather Clause is overturned in *Guinn v. United States.*

On July 28, the United States begins a 19-year occupation of Haiti, the longest in U.S. history.

In September, Carter G. Woodson founds the Association for the Study of Negro Life and History in Chicago. The association produces *The Journal of Negro History* the following year.

1916—Marcus Garvey founds the New York Division of the Universal Negro Improvement Association with 16 members. Four years later the UNIA holds its national convention in Harlem. At its height the organization claims nearly two million members.

In March the Tenth Cavalry is one of two cavalry units under the command of General John J. Pershing given the assignment to capture Mexican Revolutionary leader Pancho Villa. The Seventh Cavalry is the other. They are unsuccessful.

On July 25, Garrett Morgan uses his newly invented gas mask to rescue 32 men trapped after an explosion in a tunnel 250 feet beneath Lake Erie.

1917—The United States enters World War I on April 6. Some 370,000 African Americans join the armed forces with more than half serving in the French war zone. Over 1,000 black officers command these troops. The French government awards the *Croix de Guerre* to 107 African-American soldiers.

The East St. Louis Race Riot begins on July 1 and continues to July 3. Forty people are killed, hundreds more injured, and 6,000 driven from their homes.

Nearly 10,000 African Americans and their supporters march down Manhattan's Fifth Avenue on July 28 as part of a "silent parade," an NAACP-organized protest against lynchings, race riots, and the denial of rights. This is the first major civil rights demonstration in the 20th century.

On August 23, a riot erupts in Houston between black soldiers and white citizens; two blacks and 11 whites are killed. Twenty-nine black soldiers are executed for participation in the riot.

In August, A. Philip Randolph and Chandler Owen found *The Messenger,* a black socialist magazine, in New York City.

On November 5, the Supreme Court in *Buchanan v. Warley* strikes down the Louisville, Kentucky, ordinance mandating segregated neighborhoods.

1918—On July 25–28, a race riot in Chester, Pennsylvania, claims five lives: three blacks and two whites.

On July 26–29, in nearby Philadelphia, another race riot breaks out killing four: three blacks and one white.

The Armistice on November 11 ends World War I. However, the northern migration of African Americans continues. By 1930 there are 1,035,000 more black Americans in the North than in 1910.

1919—The Ku Klux Klan is revived in 1915 at Stone Mountain, Georgia, and by the beginning of 1919 operates in 27 states. Eighty-three African Americans are lynched during the year, among them a number of returning soldiers still in uniform.

The West Virginia State Supreme Court rules that an African American is denied equal protection under the law if his jury has no black members.

The Second Pan African Conference, led by W.E. B. Du Bois, meets in Paris in February partly to help influence the post-war Versailles Peace Conference.

The Associated Negro Press is established by Claude A. Barnett on March 2.

The twenty-five race riots that take place throughout the nation prompt the term, "Red Summer." The largest clashes take place on May 10 in Charleston, South Carolina; July 13 in Longview, Texas; July 19–23 in Washington, DC; July 27–August 1 in Chicago; September 28 in Omaha; and October 1–3 in Elaine, Arkansas.

Claude McKay publishes "If We Must Die," considered one of the first major examples of Harlem Renaissance writing.

Father Divine founds the Peace Mission Movement at his home in Sayville, New York.

South Dakota resident Oscar Micheaux releases his first film, *The Homesteader*, in Chicago. Over the next four decades Micheaux will produce and direct 24 silent films and 19 sound films, making him the most prolific black filmmaker of the 20th century.

1920—Census of 1920
U.S. Population: 105,710,620
Black Population: 10,463,131 (9.9%)

The decade of the 1920s witnesses the Harlem Renaissance, a remarkable period of creativity for black writers, poets, and artists, including among others Claude McKay, Jean Toomer, Langston Hughes, and Zora Neale Hurston.

On January 16, Zeta Phi Beta Sorority is founded at Howard University.

Andrew "Rube" Foster leads the effort to establish the Negro National (Baseball) League on February 14 in Kansas City. Eight teams are part of the league.

On August 26, the 19th Amendment to the Constitution is ratified, giving all women the right to vote. Nonetheless, African-American women, like African-American men, are denied the franchise in most southern states.

1921—On May 31–June 1, at least 60 blacks and 21 whites are killed in a race riot in Tulsa, Oklahoma. The violence destroys a thriving African-American neighborhood and business district called Deep Greenwood.

In June Sadie Tanner Mossell Alexander of the University of Pennsylvania, Eva B. Dykes of Radcliff, and Georgiana R. Simpson of the University of Chicago become the first African-American women to earn Ph.D. degrees.

Bessie Coleman, the first black female pilot, also becomes the first woman to receive an international pilot's license when she graduates from the *Federation Aeronautique International* in France.

Harry Pace forms Black Swan Phonograph Corporation, the first African-American-owned record company in Harlem. His artists will include Mamie and Bessie Smith.

One of the earliest exhibitions of work by African-American artists, including Henry Ossawa Tanner and Meta Vaux Warrick Fuller, is held at the 135th Street branch of the New York Public Library.

1922—*Shuffle Along* by Noble Sissle and Eubie Blake opens on Broadway on May 23. This is the first major play of the Harlem Renaissance.

In September William Leo Hansberry of Howard University teaches the first course in African history and civilization at an American university.

Sigma Gamma Rho Sorority is founded on November 12 in Indianapolis, Indiana.

The Harmon Foundation is established in New York City to promote African-American participation in the fine arts.

1923—On January 4, the small, predominately black town of Rosewood, Florida, is destroyed by a mob of white residents from nearby communities.

Marcus Garvey is imprisoned for mail fraud. He is sent to the Federal Penitentiary in Atlanta in 1925.

In September, the Cotton Club opens in Harlem.

Bessie Smith signs with Columbia Records to produce "race" records. Two years later she records *St. Louis Blues* with Louis Armstrong.

On November 20, Garrett T. Morgan patents the traffic signal.

The National Urban League publishes its first issue of *Opportunity, A Journal of Negro Life*. The magazine, edited by Charles S. Johnson, quickly becomes a forum for artists and authors of the Harlem Renaissance.

1924—Eugene O'Neill's play *The Emperor Jones* opens in London with Paul Robeson in the title role.

Photographer James Vander Zee begins his career by capturing images of Marcus Garvey and the UNIA.

Opera star Roland Hayes becomes the first African American to perform at Carnegie Hall in New York City.

1925—Alain Locke's *The New Negro* is published in New York City.

The National Bar Association, an organization of black attorneys, is established on August 1 in Des Moines, Iowa.

On August 2, the Brotherhood of Sleeping Car Porters and Maids is organized with A. Philip Randolph as its first president.

On September 9, Ossian Sweet, a Detroit physician, is arrested for murder after he and his family kill a member of a white mob while defending their home. The Sweet family is represented at their trial by Clarence Darrow and acquitted of the charge.

1926—Carter G. Woodson establishes Negro History Week in February between the Lincoln and Washington birthdays.

Dr. Mordecai Johnson becomes the first African-American president of Howard University in September.

The Carnegie Corporation purchases Arturo Schomburg's collection of books and artifacts on African-American life. The collection becomes the basis for the Schomburg Center for Research in Black Culture in New York City.

1927—New York businessman Abe Saperstein forms the Harlem Globetrotters basketball team on January 30.

On December 2, Marcus Garvey is deported from the United States.

1928—On November 6, Oscar DePriest, a Republican, is elected to Congress from Chicago's South Side. He is the first African American to represent a northern, urban district.

The Atlanta *Daily World* begins publication in November.

1929—Fats Waller's *Ain't Misbehavin'* opens on Broadway.

1930—Census of 1930
U.S. Population: 122,775,046
Black Population: 11,891,143 (9.7%)

James V. Herring establishes the Howard University Gallery of Art, the first gallery in the United States directed and controlled by African Americans. It is also one of the earliest galleries to highlight African-American art.

Wallace Fard Muhammad founds the Black Muslim movement in Detroit in 1930. Four years later Elijah Muhammad assumes control of the movement and transfers the headquarters to Chicago.

1931—Walter White is named NAACP executive secretary. Soon afterwards the NAACP mounts a new strategy primarily using lawsuits to end racial discrimination.

The Scottsboro Boys are arrested in Alabama. Their trial begins on April 6.

1932—The Tuskegee Syphilis Experiment begins under the direction of the U.S. Public Health Service. The experiment ends in 1972.

Gospel composer Thomas Dorsey writes "Take My Hand, Precious Lord."

Franklin Delano Roosevelt is elected president of the United States in November.

The Los Angeles *Sentinel* is founded by Leon H. Washington.

Dudley Murphy releases the film *The Emperor Jones* starring Paul Robeson.

1933—On January 31, Etta Moten becomes the first African-American entertainer to perform at the White House. She appears before President Herbert Hoover and his family in the final weeks of his administration.

1934—W.E.B. Du Bois resigns from the NAACP in a dispute over the strategy of the organization in its campaign against racial discrimination. Roy Wilkins becomes the new editor of *Crisis* magazine.

The Southern Tenant Farmers Union is organized by the Socialist Party.

Zora Neale Hurston's first novel, *Jonah's Gourd Vine,* is published.

The Apollo Theater opens in Harlem.

1935—March 20, a one-day riot erupts in Harlem, leaving two people dead.

On April 1, the U.S. Supreme Court rules in *Norris v. Alabama* that a defendant has a right to trial by a jury of his or her peers.

The Michigan *Chronicle* is founded in Detroit by Louis E. Martin.

On October 3, Italy invades Ethiopia.

On November 5, the Maryland Supreme Court rules in *Murray v. Pearson* that the University of Maryland must admit African Americans to its law school or establish a separate school for blacks. The University of Maryland chooses to admit its first black students.

On December 24, Mary McLeod Bethune calls together the leaders of 28 national women's organizations to Washington, DC, to found the National Council of Negro Women.

1936—The first meeting of the National Negro Congress takes place in Chicago on February 14, 1936. Nearly 600 black organizations are represented.

On June 24, Mary McLeod Bethune is named Director of the Division of Negro Affairs, the National Youth Administration. She is the highest-ranking black official in the Roosevelt administration and leads the Black Cabinet. She is also the first black woman to receive a presidential appointment.

Track star Jesse Owens wins four gold medals at the Berlin Olympics between August 3 and August 9.

Dr. William Augustus Hinton's book, *Syphilis and Its Treatment,* is the first published medical textbook written by an African American.

1937—William H. Hastie, former advisor to President Franklin Roosevelt, is confirmed on March 26 as the first black federal judge after his appointment by Roosevelt to the federal bench in the Virgin Islands.

The Brotherhood of Sleeping Car Porters and Maids is recognized by the Pullman Company.

Approximately 80 African Americans are among the 3,000 U.S. volunteers who fight in the Spanish Civil War. One of them, Oliver Law of Chicago, commands the Lincoln Battalion. Law is killed in battle on July 9.

On June 22, boxer Joe Louis wins the heavyweight championship in a bout with James J. Braddock in Chicago.

In October, Katherine Dunham forms the Negro Dance Group, a company of black artists dedicated to presenting aspects of African-American and African-Caribbean Dance. The company eventually becomes the Katherine Dunham Group.

1938—On June 22, Joe Louis beats Max Schmeling in a rematch of his 1936 defeat by the German boxer.

Jacob Lawrence holds his first solo exhibition at the Harlem YMCA and completes his *Toussaint L'Ouverture* series.

In November Crystal Bird Fauset of Philadelphia becomes the first African-American woman elected to a state legislature when she is chosen to serve in the Pennsylvania House of Representatives.

On December 12, the U.S. Supreme Court in *Missouri ex rel. Gaines v. Canada* rules that a state that provides in-state education for whites must provide comparable in-state education for blacks.

1939—Popular contralto Marian Anderson sings at the Lincoln Memorial before 75,000 people on Easter Sunday after the Daughters of the American Revolution refuse to allow her to perform at Constitution Hall.

Bill "Bojangles" Robinson organizes the Black Actors Guild.

World War II begins in Europe on September 1 when Germany invades Poland.

Jane M Bolin becomes the first African-American woman judge in the United States when she is appointed to the domestic relations court of New York City.

1940—Census of 1940
  U.S. Population 131,669,275
  Black Population: 12,865,518 (9.8%)

On February 29, Hattie McDaniel receives an Oscar® for Best Supporting Actress in her role in *Gone With the Wind*. She becomes the first black actor to win an Academy Award™.

Richard Wright publishes his first novel, *Native Son.*

Dr. Charles R. Drew presents his thesis, "Banked Blood," at Columbia-Presbyterian Medical Center in New York. The thesis includes his research, which discovers that plasma can replace whole blood transfusions.

In October, Benjamin Oliver Davis is named the first African-American general in the regular army.

1941—Mary Lucinda Dawson founds the National Negro Opera Company.

The U.S. Army creates the Tuskegee Air Squadron.

On June 25, Executive Order 8802 desegregates war production plants and creates the Fair Employment Practices Committee (FEPC).

On December 8, the United States enters World War II following the attack on Pearl Harbor. Dorie Miller is awarded the Navy Cross for his heroism during that battle.

1941–1945—The desperate need for factory labor to build the war machine required to win World War II leads to an unprecedented migration of African Americans from the South to the North and West. This migration transforms American politics as blacks increasingly vote in their new homes and put pressure on Congress to protect civil rights throughout the nation. Their activism lays much of the foundation for the national Civil Rights Movement a decade later.

1942—Margaret Walker publishes *For My People.*

The Congress of Racial Equality (CORE) is founded in Chicago by James Farmer, Jr., George Houser, and Bernice Fisher.

The U.S. Marine Corps accepts African-American men for the first time.

Charity Adams becomes the first black-commissioned officer in the Women's Army Auxiliary Corps (WAACs).

1943—The Naval Academy at Annapolis and other naval officer schools accept African-American men for the first time.

The Detroit Race Riot, June 20–21, claims 34 lives, including 25 African Americans. Other riots occur in Harlem; Mobile, Alabama; and Beaumont, Texas.

The first black cadets graduate from the Army Flight School at Tuskegee Institute, Alabama.

By summer, 14,000 African-American soldiers of the 93rd Infantry Division and the 32nd and 33rd companies of the Women's Army Auxiliary Corps (approximately 300 women) are stationed in the Arizona desert at Fort Huachuca for training. They are the largest concentration of black military personnel in the history of the nation.

Two American Navy Destroyer ships, the *USS Mason* and the submarine chaser *PC1264,* are staffed entirely by African-American crews.

The black 99th Pursuit Squadron (Tuskegee Airmen) flies its first combat mission in Italy.

1944—On April 3, the U.S. Supreme Court in *Smith v. Allwright* declares white-only political primaries unconstitutional.

Frederick Douglass Patterson establishes the United Negro College Fund on April 25th to help support black colleges and black students.

Rev. Adam Clayton Powell, pastor of the Abyssinian Baptist Church in New York, is elected to Congress from Harlem in November.

Gunnar Myrdal publishes *An American Dilemma*.

1945—President Franklin Delano Roosevelt dies on April 12.

The United Nations is founded at San Francisco on April 25.

On May 8, Germany surrenders on VE day.

Colonel Benjamin O. Davis, Jr., is named commander of Goodman Field, Kentucky. He is the first African American to command a military base.

Japan surrenders on VJ day, ending World War II on September 2. By the end of the war one million African-American men and women have served in the U.S. military.

Nat King Cole becomes the first African American to have a radio variety show. The show airs on NBC.

Ebony magazine publishes its first issue on November 1.

1946—Dr. Charles S. Johnson becomes the first African-American president of Fisk University.

The U.S. Supreme Court in *Morgan v. Virginia* rules that segregation in interstate bus travel is unconstitutional.

1947—On April 10, Jackie Robinson of the Brooklyn Dodgers becomes the first African American to play major league baseball in the 20th century.

The NAACP petition on racism, "An Appeal to the World," is presented to the United Nations.

1948—On July 26, President Harry Truman issues Executive Order 9981 directing the desegregation of the armed forces.

Alice Coachman becomes the first African-American woman to win an Olympic Gold Medal. She wins the high-jump competition in the London Olympics.

On October 1, the California Supreme Court voids the law banning interracial marriages in the state.

1949—In June Wesley Brown becomes the first African American to graduate from the Naval Academy at Annapolis.

Businessman Jesse Blanton, Sr., establishes WERD-AM, the first black-owned radio station. It begins broadcasting in Atlanta on October 3.

1950—Census of 1950
    U.S. Population: 150,697,361
    Black Population: 15,044,937 (10%)

On May 1, Gwendolyn Brooks of Chicago becomes the first African American to receive a Pulitzer Prize. She wins the prize in Poetry.

On September 22, Ralph Bunche becomes the first African-American recipient of a Nobel Peace Prize for his mediation of a settlement between Arabs and Israelis in the 1947–48 Mideast Crisis.

1951—On May 24, the U.S. Supreme Court rules racial segregation in District of Columbia restaurants is unconstitutional.

On May 24, a mob of 3,500 whites attempt to prevent a black family from moving into a Cicero, Illinois, apartment. Illinois Governor Adlai Stevenson calls out the Illinois National Guard to protect the family and restore order.

Harry T. Moore, a Florida NAACP official, is killed by a bomb in Mims, Florida, on December 25.

1952—Tuskegee Institute reports no lynchings in the United States for the first time in 71 years of tabulation.

Col. Benjamin O. Davis, Jr., is appointed commander of the 51st Fighter Interceptor Wing in Korea.

Ralph Ellison publishes *Invisible Man.*

1953—On June 19, in Baton Rouge, Louisiana, African Americans begin a boycott of their city's segregated municipal bus line.

On December 31, Hulan Jack becomes the first African-American borough president of Manhattan. At the time he is the highest-ranking black elected official in the nation.

1954—On May 17, the Supreme Court in *Brown v. Board of Education* declares segregation in all public schools in the United States unconstitutional, nullifying the earlier judicial doctrine of "separate but equal."

On October 27, Benjamin Oliver Davis, Jr., becomes the first black Air Force General. He also becomes the first African American to command an airbase.

Malcolm X becomes Minister of the Nation of Islam's Harlem Temple 7.

1955—Fourteen-year-old Chicago resident Emmett Till is lynched in Money, Mississippi, on August 28.

Chuck Berry, an early breakthrough rock and roll artist, records "Maybellene."

Rosa Parks refuses to relinquish her bus seat to a white man on December 1, initiating the Montgomery Bus Boycott. Soon afterwards Dr. Martin Luther King, Jr., becomes the leader of the boycott.

1956—Autherine Lucy is admitted to the University of Alabama on February 3rd. She is suspended on February 7 after a riot ensues at the university to protest her presence. Lucy is expelled on February 29.

On November 11, Nat King Cole becomes the first African American to host a primetime variety show on national television. He appears on NBC.

On November 13, the U.S. Supreme Court in *Gayle v. Browder* bans segregation in intrastate travel, effectively giving a victory to those supporting the Montgomery Bus Boycott.

1957—Congress passes the Civil Rights Act of 1957, the first legislation protecting black rights since Reconstruction. The act establishes the Civil Rights section of the Justice Department and empowers federal prosecutors to obtain court injunctions against interference with the right to vote. It also creates the federal Civil Rights Commission with the authority to investigate discriminatory conditions and recommend corrective measures.

Dorothy Irene Height is appointed president of the National Council of Negro Women, a position she holds for 41 years. She later launches a crusade for justice for black women and works to strengthen the black family.

On July 6, Althea Gibson becomes the first African American to win the Women's Singles Division of the British Tennis Championship at Wimbledon.

In September President Dwight D. Eisenhower sends federal troops to Little Rock, Arkansas, to ensure the enforcement of a federal court order to desegregate Central High School and to protect nine African-American students enrolled as part of the order. The troops remain at the high school until the end of the school year.

1958—On January 12, the Southern Christian Leadership Conference (SCLC) is organized in Atlanta with Dr. Martin Luther King, Jr., as its first President.

The Alvin Ailey Dance Theatre is formed in New York.

Louis E. Lomax becomes the first African-American newscaster. He works for WNTA-TV in New York City.

1959—On January 12, Berry Gordy, Jr., founds Motown Records in Detroit.

Lorraine Hansberry's *A Raisin in the Sun* opens on March 11 with Sidney Poitier in the starring role. It is the first play by an African-American woman to be produced on Broadway.

On April 26, Mack Charles Parker is lynched near Poplarville, Mississippi.

1960—Census of 1960
    U.S. Population: 179,323,175
    Black Population: 18,871,831 (10.6%)

On February 1, 1960, four students from North Carolina Agricultural and Technical College in Greensboro begin a sit-in at Woolworth's Drug Store to protest company policy, which bans African Americans from sitting at its counters.

On April 15, 150 black and white students gather at Shaw University in Raleigh, North Carolina, to form the Student Nonviolent Coordinating Committee (SNCC).

The Civil Rights Act of 1960 is signed into law by President Dwight D. Eisenhower on May 6. The Act establishes federal inspection of local voter registration rolls and introduces penalties for anyone who obstructs a citizen's attempt to register to vote or to cast a ballot.

Track star Wilma Rudolph of Tennessee State University is the first woman to win three gold medals at the Olympic Games, which are held this year in Rome.

On November 8, Massachusetts Senator John F. Kennedy defeats Vice President Richard Nixon in one of the closest elections in history. Many observers credit African-American voters with Kennedy's narrow margin of victory.

1961—The Congress of Racial Equality organizes Freedom Rides through the Deep South.

Riots on the University of Georgia campus in September fail to prevent the enrollment of the institution's first two African-American students, Hamilton Holmes and Charlayne Hunter (Gault).

1962—Ernie Davis, a running back at Syracuse University, becomes the first African-American athlete to receive football's Heisman Trophy.

On October 1, James Meredith becomes the first black student to enroll at the University of Mississippi. On the day he enters the university, he is escorted by U.S. marshals after federal troops are sent in to suppress rioting and maintain order.

1963—Martin Luther King writes his "Letter from a Birmingham Jail" on April 16.

On May 3, Birmingham Police use dogs and fire hoses to attack civil rights demonstrators.

Despite Governor George Wallace's vow to "block the school-house door" to prevent their enrollment on June 11, Vivian Malone and James Hood register for classes at the University of Alabama. They are the first African-American students to attend the university.

James Baldwin publishes *The Fire Next Time*.

On June 12, Mississippi NAACP Field Secretary Medgar Evers is assassinated outside his home in Jackson.

Over 200,000 people gather in Washington, DC, on August 28 as part of the March on Washington, an unprecedented demonstration demanding civil rights and equal opportunity for African Americans. Dr. Martin Luther King delivers his "I Have a Dream Speech" here.

On September 15, the Sixteenth Street Baptist Church is bombed in Birmingham, Alabama, killing four girls—Addie Mae Collins, Denise McNair, Carole Robertson, and Cynthia Wesley, ages 11–14.

President John F. Kennedy is assassinated in Dallas on November 22.

1964—On January 8, President Lyndon Johnson in his first State of the Union Address "declares unconditional war on poverty in America," thus initiating a broad array of government programs designed to assist the poorest citizens of the nation, including a disproportionate number of African Americans.

Sidney Poitier wins the Academy Award for Best Actor for his performance in the film *Lilies of the Field.*

SNCC organizes the Mississippi Freedom Summer Project.

On February 25, Cassius Clay (later Muhammad Ali) wins the first of three world heavyweight championships in a bout with Sonny Liston in Miami, Florida.

On March 12, Malcolm X announces his break with the Nation of Islam and his founding of the Muslim Mosque in Harlem.

On June 21 civil rights workers James Chaney, Andrew Goodman, and Michael Schwerner are abducted and killed by terrorists in Mississippi.

The Civil Rights Act of 1964 is passed by Congress on July 2. The act bans discrimination in all public accommodations and by employers. It also establishes the Equal Employment Opportunity Commission (EEOC) to monitor compliance with the law.

The Mississippi Freedom Democratic Party (MFDP) delegation led by Fannie Lou Hamer is denied seating at the Democratic National Convention in Atlantic City in August.

On August 20, President Lyndon Johnson signs the Economic Opportunity Act, initiating the federally sponsored War on Poverty. The act includes Head Start, Upward Bound, and Volunteers in Service to America (VISTA).

On December 10, Dr. Martin Luther King, Jr., receives the Nobel Peace Prize in Stockholm, Sweden.

1965—Malcolm X is assassinated at the Audubon Ballroom in Harlem on February 21.

On March 7, six hundred Alabama civil rights activists stage a Selma-to-Montgomery protest march to draw attention to the continued denial of black voting rights in the state. The marchers are confronted by Alabama State Troopers whose attack on them at the Edmund Pettus Bridge is carried on national television. On March 21, Dr. Martin Luther King leads a five-day, 54-mile march retracing the route of the original activists. The 3,300 marchers at the beginning of the trek eventually grow to 25,000 when they reach the Alabama capitol on March 25. After the protest march, President Lyndon Johnson proposes the Voting Rights Act to guarantee black voting throughout the South.

In March, the White House releases "The Negro Family: The Case for National Action," popularly known as the Moynihan Report.

On June 4, President Lyndon Johnson first uses the term "affirmative action" in a speech at Howard University.

Alex Haley publishes the *Autobiography of Malcolm X*.

The Voting Rights Act is signed into law on August 6.

The Watts Uprising occurs on August 11–16. Thirty-four people are killed and one-thousand are injured in the five day confrontation.

Maulana Ron Karenga founds the black nationalist organization US in Los Angeles following the Watts Uprising.

1966—On January 13, Robert Weaver, President Lyndon Baines Johnson's nominee to head the newly created Department of Housing and Urban Development, is confirmed for the post by the U.S. Senate. Weaver becomes the first African American to hold a cabinet post.

On January 25th Constance Baker Motley is appointed by President Lyndon Baines Johnson to the Federal Bench in New York City. She becomes the first African-American woman elevated to a federal judgeship.

In May, Stokely Carmichael becomes chairman of SNCC and embraces the concept of "black power."

On June 5, James Meredith begins a solitary March Against Fear for 220 miles from Memphis to Jackson, Mississippi, to protest racial discrimination. Soon after crossing into Mississippi, Meredith is shot by a sniper. Civil rights leaders, including Martin Luther King (SCLC), Floyd McKissick (CORE), and Stokely Carmichael (SNCC), vow to continue the march that eventually reaches Jackson. While in Greenwood, Carmichael gives his first "Black Power" speech on June 26.

On October 15, The Black Panther Party is formed in Oakland, California, by Bobby Seale and Huey P. Newton.

Andrew F. Brimmer is appointed by President Johnson to be the first African American to serve on the Federal Reserve Board.

James T. Whitehead, Jr., becomes the first African American to pilot a U-2 spy plane.

On November 8, Edward Brooke of Massachusetts becomes the first African American to be popularly elected to the U.S. Senate.

On November 8, Julian Bond wins a seat in the Georgia State Senate. However he is denied the seat by the Georgia Legislature because of his opposition to the Vietnam War. Bond is eventually seated after a bitter court battle.

1967—On April 4, Dr. Martin Luther King, Jr., delivers "Beyond Vietnam: A Time to Break Silence" at a meeting of Clergy and Laity Concerned at Riverside Church, New York City.

H. Rap Brown becomes chairman of SNCC on May 12.

On June 12, the U.S. Supreme Court in *Loving v. Virginia* strikes down state interracial marriage bans.

The six-day Newark Riot begins on July 12 and claims 23 dead, 725 injured, and 1,500 arrested.

Thurgood Marshall takes his seat as the first African-American Justice on the United States Supreme Court on July 13.

On July 23, Detroit erupts. Between July 23 and July 28, 43 are killed, 1,189 are injured, and over 7,000 are arrested.

On November 13, Carl Stokes and Richard G. Hatcher are elected the first black mayors of Cleveland, Ohio, and Gary, Indiana, respectively.

1968—On February 8, three students at South Carolina State College in Orangeburg are killed by police in what will be known as the Orangeburg Massacre.

The Report of the National Advisory Commission on Civil Disorders, popularly known as the Kerner Report, is released in March.

Dr. Martin Luther King, Jr., is assassinated in Memphis, Tennessee, on April 4. In the wake of the assassination 125 cities in 29 states experience uprisings. By April 11, 46 people are killed and 35,000 are injured in these confrontations.

In April Congress enacts the Civil Rights Act of 1968, which outlaws discrimination in the sale and rental of housing.

New York Senator and presidential candidate Robert F. Kennedy is assassinated on June 5 in Los Angeles.

On June 19, the Poor People's Campaign brings 50,000 demonstrators to Washington, DC.

Arthur Ashe becomes the first African American to win the Men's Singles competition in the U.S. Open.

San Francisco State University establishes the nation's first Black Studies Program in September.

In November Shirley Chisholm of New York is the first black woman elected to the U.S. Congress.

1969—The Ford Foundation gives one million dollars to Morgan State University, Howard University, and Yale University to help prepare faculty members to teach courses in African-American studies.

On May 5, Moneta Sleet, Jr., of *Ebony* magazine, becomes the first African American to win a Pulitzer Prize in Photography.

On September 22, the African-American Studies Program begins offering courses at Harvard University.

Geneticist Alfred Day Hershey, Ph.D., becomes the first African American to share a Nobel Prize in Medicine when he is recognized for his work on the replication and genetic structure of viruses.

Robert Chrisman and Nathan Hare publish the first issue of *The Black Scholar* in November.

Howard N. Lee becomes the first African-American mayor of Chapel Hill, North Carolina. At the time he is the first African-American mayor of a predominately white southern city.

On December 4, Chicago police kill Black Panther leaders Fred Hampton and Mark Clarke.

1970—Census of 1970
U.S. Population: 204,765,770
Black Population: 22,580,289 (11.1%)

Dr. Clifton Wharton, Jr., is named president of Michigan State University on January 2. He is the first African American to lead a major, predominately white university.

On February 18, Bobby Seale and six other defendants (popularly known as the Chicago Seven) are acquitted of the charge of conspiring to disrupt the 1968 Democratic National Convention.

The first issue of *Essence* magazine appears in May.

On May 15, two students, Philip Lafayette Gibbs and James Earl Green, are killed by police in a confrontation with students at Jackson State University, Jackson, Mississippi.

On July 1, Kenneth Gibson becomes the first black mayor of an eastern city when he assumes the post in Newark, New Jersey.

The first issue of *Black Enterprise* magazine appears in August.

The San Rafael, California, courthouse shooting on August 7 results in the death of Judge Harold Haley and three others, including Jonathan Jackson, the younger brother of imprisoned Black Panther George Jackson. UCLA Philosophy Professor Angela Davis is implicated in the shooting and becomes the subject of a nationwide FBI-led search. Davis is captured and brought to trial. She is acquitted of all charges on June 4, 1972.

On October 12, Charles Gordone becomes the first African American to win a Pulitzer Prize in Drama for his play, *No Place to Be Somebody.*

The Joint Center for Political Studies is established in Washington, DC.

1971—On January 12th the Congressional Black Caucus is formed in Washington, DC.

In July Captain Samuel L. Gravely, Jr., is promoted to Rear Admiral. He becomes the first African American to achieve Flag Rank in the U.S. Navy.

On September 9, nearly 1,200 inmates seize control of half of the New York State Prison at Attica. Four days later 29 inmates and ten hostages are killed when state troopers and correctional officers suppress the uprising.

On December 18, Rev. Jesse Jackson founds People United to Save Humanity (PUSH) in Chicago.

1972—On March 10–12, several thousand African Americans gather in Gary, Indiana, for the first National Black Political Convention.

Over the summer New York Congresswoman Shirley Chisholm makes an unsuccessful bid for the Democratic presidential nomination. She is the first African American to campaign for the nomination.

In November Barbara Jordan of Houston and Andrew Young of Atlanta become the first black Congressional representatives elected from the South since 1898.

The first Haitian "boat people" arrive in south Florida.

1973—On May 29, Thomas Bradley is elected the first black mayor of Los Angeles in the modern era. He is reelected four times and thus holds the mayor's office for 20 years.

The National Black Feminist Organization is established with Margaret Sloan-Hunter elected as its chair.

Marian Wright Edelman creates the Children's Defense Fund.

On October 16, Maynard H. Jackson, Jr., is elected the first black mayor of Atlanta.

On November 6, Coleman Young is elected the first black mayor of Detroit.

1974—On April 8, Henry "Hank" Aaron hits his 715th home run to become the all-time leader in home runs in major league baseball.

On June 21, U.S. District Judge W. Arthur Garrity initiates a busing program, involving several thousand students, designed to desegregate the public schools of Boston.

The largest single gift to date from a black organization is the $132,000 given by the Links, Inc., to the United Negro College Fund on July 1.

On October 30, Muhammad Ali defeats George Foreman in Kinshasa, Zaire, to regain the world heavyweight championship.

On November 5, George Brown and Mervyn Dymally are elected Lieutenant Governors of Colorado and California, respectively. They are the first African Americans to hold these posts in the 20th century.

1975—The Morehouse School of Medicine (Atlanta) becomes the only black medical school established in the United States in the 20th century. The first dean and president of Morehouse School of Medicine is Dr. Louis Sullivan, who later becomes the Secretary of the U.S. Department of Health and Human Services.

Wallace D. Muhammad assumes control of the Nation of Islam after the death of his father, Elijah Muhammad. He changes the organization's direction and its name to the World Community of al-Islam.

Arthur Ashe becomes the first African American to win the British Men's Singles at Wimbledon.

General Daniel "Chappie" James of the Air Force becomes the first African-American four-star general.

The first black-owned television station, WGPR, begins broadcasting in Detroit.

On October 12, Frank Robinson becomes the first black Major League Baseball manager when he takes over the Cleveland Indians.

1976—The United States Naval Academy at Annapolis admits women for the first time in June. Janie L. Mines becomes the first African-American woman cadet to enter. She graduates in 1980.

College and university enrollment for African-American students rises sharply, from 282,000 in 1966 to 1,062,000 in 1976.

1977—In January, Patricia Roberts Harris is appointed by President Jimmy Carter to head the Housing and Urban Development Department. She becomes the first African-American woman to hold a cabinet position.

In January, Congressman Andrew Young is appointed by President Carter to be U.S. Ambassador to the United Nations. He is the first African American to hold that post.

The eighth and final night for the miniseries based on Alex Haley's *Roots* is shown on February 3. This final episode achieves the highest ratings to that point for a single television program.

On March 8, Henry L. Marsh III becomes the first African-American mayor of Richmond, Virginia.

In September, Randall Robinson founds TransAfrica, a lobbying group for Africa, in Washington, DC.

1978—Minister Louis Farrakhan breaks with the World Community of al-Islam and becomes the leader of the revived Nation of Islam.

On June 28, the U.S. Supreme Court in *Regents of the University of California v. Bakke* narrowly upholds affirmative action as a legal strategy for addressing past discrimination.

On September 15, Muhammad Ali becomes the first boxer to win the heavyweight championship three times when he defeats Leon Spinks at the Superdome in New Orleans.

1979—The Sugar Hill Gang records "Rapper's Delight" in Harlem.

Franklin Thomas is named president of the Ford Foundation. He is the first African American to head a major philanthropic foundation.

Frank E. Petersen, Jr., becomes the first African American to earn the rank of General in the United States Marines.

In September Hazel W. Johnson becomes the first African-American woman to be promoted to the rank of General in the United States Army.

Richard Arrington, Jr., is elected the first African-American mayor of Birmingham, Alabama.

The Nobel Prize in Economics goes to Sir Arthur Lewis of Princeton University. He is the first black person to win the award in a category other than peace.

1980—Census of 1980
U.S. Population: 226,504,825
Black Population: 26,482,349 (11.8%)

In January Willie Lewis Brown, Jr., becomes the first African-American Speaker in a state legislature when he is selected for the post in the California Assembly. Brown holds the Speakership until 1995, when he is elected Mayor of San Francisco.

On May 17–18, rioting breaks out in Liberty City, Florida (near Miami), after police officers are acquitted for killing an unarmed black man. The riot, which generates 15 deaths, is the worst in the nation since Detroit in 1967.

Toni Cade Bambara's *The Salt Eaters* wins the American Book Award.

Robert L. Johnson begins operation of Black Entertainment Television (BET) out of Washington, DC.

1982—The struggle of Rev. Ben Chavis and his followers to block a toxic waste dump in Warren County, North Carolina, launches a national campaign against environmental racism.

Bryant Gumbel is named anchor of *The Today Show*, becoming the first African American to hold the post on a major network.

1983—On April 12, Harold Washington is elected the first black mayor of Chicago.

On August 30, Guion (Guy) S. Bluford, Jr., a crew member on the shuttle *Challenger*, becomes the first African-American astronaut to make a space flight.

Vanessa Williams becomes the first African American crowned Miss America on September 18 in Atlantic City. In July 1984 she relinquishes her crown when nude photos of her appear in *Penthouse* magazine.

On November 2, President Ronald Reagan signs a bill establishing January 20 as a federal holiday in honor of Martin Luther King, Jr.

Alice Walker's *The Color Purple* wins the Pulitzer Prize for Fiction.

Harvey Bernard Gantt becomes the first African-American mayor of Charlotte, North Carolina.

1984—On January 2, W. Wilson Goode becomes the first African-American mayor of Philadelphia.

In January Rev. Jesse Jackson travels to Syria to negotiate the release of U.S. Air Force pilot Robert Goodman who had been shot down over that country. Jackson returns to the United States with the freed pilot.

Rev. Jesse Jackson wins approximately one-fourth of the votes cast in the Democratic primaries and caucuses and about one-eighth of the convention delegates in a losing bid for the Democratic presidential nomination.

In August Carl Lewis wins four gold medals at the Olympics in Los Angeles, matching the record set by Jesse Owens in 1936.

In September *The Cosby Show* makes its television debut. The show runs for eight seasons and will become the most successful series in television history featuring a mostly African-American cast.

Russell Simmons forms Def Jam Records in Harlem.

1985—In May, Philadelphia's African-American mayor, Wilson Goode, orders the Philadelphia police to bomb the headquarters of MOVE, a local black nationalist organization. The bombing leaves 11 people dead and 250 homeless.

1986—On January 20, the first national Martin Luther King, Jr., holiday is celebrated.

On January 28, Dr. Ronald McNair and six other crew members die when the space shuttle *Challenger* explodes shortly after launch from the Kennedy Space Center in Florida.

The Oprah Winfrey Show becomes nationally syndicated.

Spike Lee releases his first feature film, *She's Gotta Have It*, initiating a new wave of interest in black films and African-American filmmakers.

1987—Rita Dove wins the Pulitzer Prize for poetry.

On August 6, Reginald Lewis orchestrates the leveraged buyout of Beatrice Foods to become the first African-American CEO of a billion-dollar corporation.

Neurosurgeon Dr. Ben Carson makes medical history when he leads a seventy-member surgical team at Johns Hopkins Hospital in a 22-hour operation separating Siamese twins (the Binder twins) joined at the cranium.

On October 28, Brigadier General Fred A. Gordon is appointed Commandant of the Cadets at the U.S. Military Academy at West Point.

On December 8, Kurt Lidell Schmoke becomes the first African-American mayor of Baltimore elected by popular vote.

1988—In his second try for the Democratic presidential nomination, Jesse L. Jackson receives 1,218 delegate votes at the Democratic National Convention on July 20. The number needed for the nomination, which goes to Michael Dukakis, is 2,082.

In September, Temple University offers the first Ph.D. degree in African-American Studies.

On November 4, comedian Bill Cosby announces his gift of $20 million to Spelman College. This is the largest donation ever made by a black American to a college or university.

1989—On January 29, Barbara Harris is elected the first woman bishop of the Episcopal Church.

On February 7, Ronald H. Brown is elected chair of the Democratic National Committee, becoming the first African American to head one of the two major political parties.

In March Frederick Drew Gregory becomes the first African American to command a space shuttle when he leads the crew of *Discovery.*

Houston, Texas, Congressman George Thomas "Mickey" Leland is killed in a plane crash near Gambela, Ethiopia, on August 7.

On August 10, General Colin L. Powell is named chair of the U. S. Joint Chiefs of Staff, the first African American to hold the post.

On November 7, L. Douglas Wilder wins the governorship of Virginia, making him the first African American to be popularly elected to that office. On the same day David Dinkins and Norm Rice are the first African Americans elected as mayors of New York and Seattle, respectively.

1990—Census of 1990
U.S. Population: 248,709,878
Black Population: 29,986,060 (12%)

On February 11, Nelson Mandela, South African Black Nationalist, is freed after 27 years in prison.

August Wilson wins a Pulitzer Prize for the play *The Piano Lesson*.

In November Sharon Pratt Kelly is elected mayor of Washington, DC. She becomes the first African-American woman to lead a large American city.

1991—On January 15, Roland Burris becomes the first black attorney general of Illinois.

On March 3, Los Angeles police use force to arrest Rodney King after a San Fernando Valley traffic stop. The beating of King is captured on videotape and broadcast widely, prompting an investigation and subsequent trial of three officers.

On April 10, Emanuel Cleaver II is sworn in as the first African-American mayor of Kansas City, Missouri.

On June 18, Wellington Webb becomes the first African-American mayor of Denver, Colorado.

On October 23, Federal Judge Clarence Thomas, nominated by President George H.W. Bush, is confirmed by the U.S. Senate and takes his seat on the U.S. Supreme Court.

Julie Dash releases *Daughters of the Dust,* the first feature film by an African-American woman.

1992—In March Willie W. Herenton is elected the first African-American mayor of Memphis, Tennessee.

On April 29, a Simi Valley, California, jury acquits the three officers accused of beating Rodney King. The verdict triggers a three-day uprising in Los Angeles that results in over 50 people killed, over 2,000 injured, and 8,000 arrested.

On September 12, Dr. Mae Carol Jemison becomes the first African-American woman in space when she travels on board the space shuttle *Endeavour.*

On November 3, Carol Moseley Braun of Illinois becomes the first African-American woman elected to the United States Senate.

1993—In April Freeman Robertson Bosley, Jr., becomes the first African-American mayor of St. Louis, Missouri.

M. Joycelyn Elders becomes the first African American and the first woman to be named United States Surgeon General on September 7.

On October 7, Toni Morrison becomes the first black American to win the Nobel Prize in Literature. The work honored is her novel *Beloved.*

1994—On June 12, O.J. Simpson's former wife, Nicole Brown Simpson, and her friend Ronald Goldman are found stabbed to death. O.J. Simpson emerges as the leading suspect and is subsequently arrested on June 17 after a two-hour, low-speed pursuit of Simpson and his friend Al Cowlings that is seen on television by an estimated 95 million people.

1995—On October 3, after an eight-month televised trial, O.J. Simpson is acquitted of the charges of murder in the deaths of Nicole Brown Simpson and Ronald Goldman.

On May 6, Ron Kirk wins the mayoral race in Dallas, becoming the first African-American mayor of the city.

The Million Man March organized by Minister Louis Farrakhan is held in Washington, DC, on October 17.

Dr. Helene Doris Gayle becomes the first woman and the first African-American Director of the National Center for HIV, STD, and TB Prevention for the U.S. Centers for Disease Control.

1996—Commerce Secretary Ron Brown is killed in a plane crash near Dubrovnik, Croatia, on April 3.

On April 9, George Walker becomes the first African American to win a Pulitzer Prize for Music. The winning composition, *Lilies for Soprano or Tenor and Orchestra*, is based on a poem by Walt Whitman.

In May, President Bill Clinton signs into law the Personal Responsibility and Work Opportunity Reconciliation Act, which replaces the Aid to Families with Dependent Children (AFDC) with state block grants. It also substantially cuts programs designed to help the poor.

On November 5, California voters pass Proposition 209, which outlaws affirmative action throughout the state.

1997—On April 13, golfer Tiger Woods wins the Master's Tournament in Augusta, Georgia. At 21 he is the youngest golfer ever to win the title. He is also the first African American to hold the title.

In June, Harvey Johnson, Jr., is sworn in as the first black mayor of Jackson, Mississippi.

On October 25 African-American women participate in the Million Woman March in Philadelphia, focusing on healthcare, education, and self-help.

In December, Lee Patrick Brown becomes Houston's first African-American mayor.

1998—On June 7, churchgoers discover the dismembered body of James Byrd, Jr., in Jasper, Texas. It is later determined that three white supremacists chained Byrd, who is black, to the back of a pick-up truck and dragged him to his death.

1999—On January 13, after thirteen seasons and six NBA championships, professional basketball star Michael Jordan retires from the game as a player.

On September 10, Serena Williams wins the U.S. Open Women's Singles Tennis Championship.

2000—Census of 2000
  U.S. Population: 281,421,906
  Black Population: 34,658,190 (12.3%)

Rev. Vashti M. McKenzie becomes the first woman bishop of the African Methodist Episcopal Zion Church.

Timeline: 2001–

2001—In January President-elect George Bush nominates Colin Powell to be Secretary of State. Condoleezza Rice takes the position of National Security Advisor for the Bush administration. This is the first time either of these posts is held by an African American.

In November Shirley Clarke Franklin becomes the first African-American woman to head the government of a major southern city when she is elected mayor of Atlanta.

2002—In March, Halle Berry and Denzel Washington win Oscars for best actress and best actor for their portrayals in *Monster's Ball* and *Training Day,* respectively.

2004—On November 2, Barack Obama is elected to the U.S. Senate from Illinois. He becomes the second African American elected to the Senate from that state, and only the fifth black U.S. Senator in history.

2005—In January Condoleezza Rice becomes the Secretary of State. She is the first African-American woman to hold the post.

On August 30, Hurricane Katrina hits the Gulf Coast, taking an estimated 1,700 lives. The vast majority of the deaths are in Louisiana, including heavily African-American New Orleans.

2006—The *Covenant with Black America* text, edited by Tavis Smiley, climbs to number 1 on the *New York Times Book Review* bestseller list, making it the first book published by a black publisher to reach number 1 on the nonfiction paperback list.

Deval Patrick is elected Governor of Massachusetts. He becomes the second African American in the nation popularly elected to this position.

With the Democratic takeover of both the U.S. House of Representatives and Senate in the November midterm elections, for the first time at least three members of the Congressional Black Caucus will chair full committees in the House.

APPENDIX III:
THAT'S MY BABY!

The cover art for THE COVENANT *In Action* is an original creation by Martin O. Erb of ERBan Associates (**www.erban.com**).

The wraparound cover of images, representing the future of Black America, is comprised of 499 photographs featuring 605 African-American babies. These images were submitted by black folk from all four corners of America.

When you log onto **www.covenantwithblackamerica.com**, you can click on the individual baby's image to learn more about him or her.

Here now are the names provided to us of the babies so lovingly portrayed on the cover of THE COVENANT *In Action*.

A–G

Miles Agee; Merideth Alexander; Jeffrey Allen, II; Kecia L. Allen; Kiarra Makeda Alleyne; Joshua Allison; Kayla Anderson; Sydney Armstrong; LaCrystal Artis; Anansa Ashanti; Makahia Askew; Cliff, Shannon, and Stacey Avery; Yanni, Desean, and Nia Baker; Donald Bandy; Cydney Banks; Areanna Barber; Kristian Barber; Adrian and Andrew Barker; Reighan Barnes; Kayla and Joshua Barney; David Bass; Zakai Beach; Lauren and Leah Bennett; Alec and Jasmine Betts; Kaili Beverly; Julian Billinger; Cario White-Kahrontai Bledsoe; Jailyn and Jaedyn Bolton; Amare Bond; Marcus Boone; Alyssa Nicole Bowser; Trinity Kelise Brooks; Ahmani Brown; Brenda Brown and Larry Naylor; Eric J. Brown; Immanuel King Brown; Nevaeh Brown; Courtney Buggs; Ahmir and Keshaun Bunkley; Joshua Burks; Kennedy Elizabeth Burnett; Quiana Butler; K. Eddie Bynum; Sonya Bynum; Avery Cane; Mason and Matthew Cardwell; Jasmine Danae Carolina; Karen Carter; Keilah A. Causey; Emerleysha Stacy Charles; Jasmine Chatman; Justin Cheatham; Ashton Chuney; McKenzie Claiborne; Trinity Clancy; Danielle Clark; Dominique Clark; Kendsey Clark; Candace Joy Clemons; Kendall Paulette Cochran; Zoie Colbert; Joshua Cole; Haile and Gabby Cooper; Miya Cottoms; Jaden Cousin; Layken Cowley; Jaden Croone; DeJujuan Darden; Kyra and Micah Deams; Ellen DeJarnett; Elijah Anthony Dendy; Keith Dickens; Justin Dobson; Boston Dorch; Rodney Dorsey, Jr.; Inayah Ameere Drewery; Kayla Drumgo; Laya Dupri; Tyler Duane Eaden; Olivia East; Kearsten Edwards; Tyler Edwards; Bria and

Tia Elder; Kendi Ella; Lyndsey, Brittany, and Cory Elliott; Bryan Ellis; Jordan Endsley, Dee Dee Johnson, and Julius Endsley; Jadon Dominic Evans; Aubri Fairley; Charles Farrow, III; Tinia and Tatiana Farrow; Jaylyn Madisen Ferrell; Tenille Fields; Mia Flowers; Terence Foxx; Michael Immanuel Franklin; Kyra K.E. Freeman; Micheal Fuller; Amber J. Galloway; Maiya Gardner; Nevell and Richan Gaskins; Chandler M. Gates; Keanu Gibbons; DeJon Gibbs, Jr.; Langston Glaude; Jace Glover; Autumn Marie Graves; Destiny Graves; Tony Graves; Malik A. Green; Anaiah Symone Greene; Kyle Aubrey Greene, Jr.; Ania Greer; Adira Rene and Tariq Caleb Griffin; Kerry T. N. Grooms; Kaiden Guillory; Spencer, Steven, Jr., and Desiré Guillory

H–O

Riccardo, Jordan, and Janae Haley; Tielle Hall; Deirdre and Eric Hammons; Nick Hampton; Kynnedy, Destiny, Kayla, and Donovan Hardaway; Dalyn Makhi Harden; Darrell Harden; Aaliyah Sierra Harris; DeAndre Harris; Kayla Lauryn Harris; Rileigh Kaitlyn Harvey; Yuka, Ayana, and Elijah Hatcher; Gianna Hawkins; De'Shyne Hayes; Jerresha Haynes; Naila Haynes; Christian Herndon; Kayla Ledrea Hewins; Kelvin Lebrone Hewins; Dionte Darius Hicks; Rozaria Higgins; Mikki Allen Hill; Malcolm X, Bailey, and Jordan Hodge; Jordan Holley; Erica Holloman; Isabel Walker Holmes; Adam B. Humphrey, Jr.; Elizabeth Marie Hunter; Myeva Jeanine Hurte; Clinton and Caila Jackson; Laiya Jackson; Myles Jackson; Camron James; Amirah Jenkins; Isoke Jenkins-Dyer, Lonnie-Scott Holden, and Jasmine Mitchell Holden; Brandon Jennings; Angela C. Johnson; Carmella, Adrienne, Larry, and Jasmine Johnson, with Eboni and Andre Harris; Cyrus Quinten Johnson; Eric and Jada Johnson; Genesis Johnson; Jaleel and Jason Johnson; Joshua C. Johnson-Reed; Lena Rene Brown Johnson; Nyrene and Nylea Johnson; Patrick B. Johnson, Jr.; Rodd Evan Johnson; Kalista Jones; Mary N. Whigham Jones; Nicholas Jones; Kaylin Alexandria and Cameron Alexander Jordan; Griffen Joyner; Gerald Kameryn; Ashaiyt Ma'at Kara; Sterling and Spencer Kee; Kristopher Kelley; Cassidy Kemp-Gary; Jennifer Keown; Aiyoni King; Terrolyn Kissai; Wilson Lane, III; Kadence Aldonyea Lang; Lauren Monai Lavender; Imani Maya LeBon; Simone Azure Lenoir; Delton Lewis; Eliason Lewis; Kolbi Lockwood; Davion Lofton; Andrew Ray Love; Darius McCoy; Reggie McDonald; Jamesha McFadden; Nadia Gayle McGahee; Chazmine McKelvey; Brooke Maginley; Kennedy Manning; Landen Antonio Manuel; Jayla Mapp; Kacey Mariah; Kelin Lorenzo Mark, Jr.; Sydney Marshall; Ke'Juan

Martin; Darius Mata; Alaysia Nichelle Mathis; Dasia May; Destinee Seania Mayes; Brandy and Tommie Middleton; Constance Miller; Jocelyn S. Miller; Tamika Miller; Dexter A. Mitchell II; Monica Monet and Mysun Kidd; Andrew Darin Moore; Donna Moore; Chase and Shawn Morgan, Jr.; Amber Murray; Chelsea Marie Orlean Muskelly; Lydia, Lauryn, and Layna Myrick; Richie Myrick; Eric Neal II; Khoran Jelani Newell; Amari Nicole Nicholson; T. Ray Jemar Noble; O'llura O'bannon; Aria Joi Obey; Braxton Offor; Kelva Renee' Olds; Kyler and Kennedy Owens

P–Z

Meghan Parker; Quiran Parker; Kelsey B. Parks; Kenzi Curette Patton; Treasure Pearson; Amya Sofia and Autumn Nicole Perez; Angie, Amanda, and Adam Perry; Madison Phillips; Lekeisha Dy'Anne Pittman; William, Diana, Maya, Dara, and Jana Prentiss; Louis and Alexis Preston; Savannah Lynn Prince; Ciara Pryor; Reese and Kai Revere; Kaelyn and Kelsey Rice; Brittany Roger; Asha S. Roland; Darreyon Rosser; Madyson R. Spaulding Rosser; Taylor Symone and Tiyah Jayde Saulter; Samuel Johnathan Scarborough; Laryn and Archie Scott, Jr.; Madison S. Scott; Perry Edmond and Paul Anthony Scott; Jayden Parker Seaton; Ariel R. Seltzer; Gordon Shaw, Jr.; Princess Shea; Kyler Shorter; Dylan and Davyn Side; Kaylyn Simmons; Winter Simmons; Erick Trey and Karah Day Simpson; Willis Joseph Singleton, Jr.; Jayvon Slater; Chelsea Marie Small; Deandra Small; Caleb Smith and Kameron Brown; Gelisa Smith; Jazmine Smith; Michelei Smith; Nicole Smith; Janai Sobers; Remi Danielle, Roderick Dale, Jr., and Rodquel La'Shun Spells; Fabian Spence; Sydney Stamps; Taylar Stamps; Jasmyn Stanley; Terrion Stearns; Gary Leo Stephens; Savannah Stephens; Tyree, Naimah, and Nafisah Stevens; Keenan and Kelise Stewart; Ashley and Richard Stokes; Kristen, Justin, and Jalen Sueing; Ronald S. "Trey" Sullivan, III; Camryn Kamill Sutton; Katia M. Sutton; Kourtland B. Tate; Janniyah Taylor; Jarra and Jay Taylor; Jordan Taylor; Keith Taylor; Seth McNair Taylor; Tyler Taylor; Micah Thigpen; Hailey Thomas; Collin Thompson; Allimah and David Thrower; LaRyiah Marie Tillman; Keyshawn Townsend; Camri Cross Treadwell; Gabriel K. Trotter; Johnathan J. Troup; Ra'Vyn Kyndall Tucker-Green; Sydney Tucker; Justin Vaden; Terri Wair; Omar, Osiah, and Orion Walker; Kayla Wall; Bianca and Justin Wallace; Nikki, Rikki, and Mila Wallace; Dante Walston; Jasminette Walston; James G. Walton II; Kristi Watkins; Jarrett and Farai Webster; Dilan Zeytun West; Adrian Weston; Olivia and Zoe Whatley; Ania Greer Wheeler; Jason Wheeler; Aiden White; Craig Ferrell White, III; Jalen White; Kamari Demyne Jaquii Whitsett; Kamari Janese Wiggins; Kassidy Wiley; Adam S. Williams; Alexis and Madisyn Williams; Chris, Jr., Christian, Cameron, and Joe Williams; Dorian Orlando Williams, II; Jonas Sebastian Williams; Kyndall Williams; Mya Williams; Vernita Williamson; Kayla Willis; Amari Wilson; Christopher Michael Wilson; Kayla Wilson; Rory Wilson; Braniya Zolay Woods and Tabitha Barber; Kelby D. Woods; Kendall Wright; Alexis Iman Young; Beverly Yvette Henshaw Young; David Lawrence Zeigler, III

❧

When Tavis Smiley put a call out for baby photographs, the response was overwhelming! Of the nearly 2,000 submissions received, we realized no more than one-fourth of them could be included in the unique wraparound cover art. Nonetheless, we did want to acknowledge the other beautiful black babies who also represent the future of Black America but who are not pictured on our cover. However, you can see their images at *The Covenant* website, **www.covenantwithblackamerica.com**. Here now are those babies, by name.

A–G

Kirstan Adams; Savion Adams; Corey Agnew; Quaran Evyn Ahmad; Antoine Alexander; Janae Alexander; Thomas Lee, IV, and Tonja Lei Simone Alexander; Patricia Ali's granddaughters Yazmine and Nadia; Allen Temple AME Youth Choir; Alyssa Allen; Brianna Marie Allen; Camryn Mariah Allen; Jordan and Malik Allen; Kendra Allen; Rhondrea Allen; David Allison; Devin T. Anderson and Uriah Jah-Mil Larry; Jared Javon Anderson; Tim Anderson, Jr.; Katie and Kyla Andrews; Laurel Elisabeth Andrews; Michael Keith Andrus, Jr.; Aaren Anthony; Lauren Z. Anthony; Tyler Anthony; Anthony M. Appleby; Hassan Armstrong; Ann Arnold; Payton Arthur Ash; Sara and Zavier Avery; Keturah Aziz; Stephanie D. Bacon; Isaiah, Kennedy, and Taylor Bailey; Natalia Bailey; Carlton Isaiah Baker; Clarissa Baker; Talia and Tari Baker (due to arrive any minute!); Aaron W. Baldwin; Carson A. Baldwin; Ellise Bailey Banks; JoVonte' Montrell Barber; Brianna Barnes; Christopher Nelson, Christen Nel'Unique, and Christione Barnes; Maya, Adrian, and Christopher Barnes; Ralph Barnes; Michael Barnett; Jamiah Bass; Xavia Batchelor and Jordan Stamps; A'Maria Carter Bates;

Ava Janiece Batson; Dameron LaBryant Batson, Jr.; Dante Lamont and Devon Lamont Baxter; Aquil F. Bayyan, Jr.; Philip Wayne, Jr., Norma Jean, Renee Alexander, and Rachelle Ann Beamon; Jalen Beck; John and Jasmine Bell; Latifa and Tanya Bell; Deja Simone Bellamy; Avery Camille Bennekin; Amarrah Sienna Bennett; Je'Neka Nisaa', Wayne, and Jasmine Bennett; Jordan and Sydney Bennett; Mylani Faith Benson; Nicole, Myles, and Mya Benson; Airi Bentley; Aaron Lee Berry; Zita Berry; Lauryn Da'Naine Bervine; Layla Bessant; Jamiel D. Best; Endeara K. Lee Bickham; Reginal Bisor and Donovan Rice; Genae Angelice Bisson; Lauran Alexandria Reese Blackwood; Hollis Blake, IV; Anthony, III, Ashanti, and JayDen Blowe; Jon Francis Bobb; Chaseton Omari Bobino; Bryan Booker, Jr.; Jaylyn, Jaydyn, and Kierra Booker; Yvette Booker; Jeremiah Dayshaun Booth; Sean DeMichael Booth; Nahji Gabriel Borden; Demarius Bounds; Jared and Ja'lean Bounds; Kyliea Bourne; Christian Bowers; Austin Pryce Boyd; Cameron, Carmen, and Courtney Bradford; Alexandria Theresa and Breanna Elizabeth Bradley; Aiden Bramwell; Mario Braswell, Jr.; Nia Lindsey Jordan Brewster; Jesse Bynum; Donna Campbell Brice's grandchildren: Morris Neeley Campbell, III, Maxwell Nicolas Campbell, Gavyn Grant Smith, Tiron Smith, and Paige Autrice Smith; Caleb A. Brinson; Jelani Britt; Sophia, Nevin, Jr., and Benjamin Brittain; Jaden Brice; Jordan Brice; Evan Charles Brooks; Leasha Brooks; Alanis "Laney" Broussard and Lauren Phillips; Fred G. Broussard, Jr.; Alana Brielle Brown; Alison Brown; Alton Brown; Aminah Brown, Rasheed Porter, and Nabilah Brown; Caleb Brown; Dylan Reece Brown; Gary Brown; Janae Brown and Jayden Goodwyn; Jordan Brown and Gabrielle Mayes; Joshua Brown; Kolby Brown; Octavia and Tavara Brown; Reagan Hannah Brown; Timmy Brown; William Elijah Louis Henry Lee Brown; Abdul Raheem Hakam Bryant, Jr.; Kenan Emory and Cayin Sheldon Bryant; Neys'san and Cairen Bryant; Symphonie Bryant-Brown, Marcus Evans, Joshua Bryant, and Jordan Dickerson; Angela, Julian, Alexander, and Tiffany Buckner; Robert Anthony Buie; Jamar Curtis Bullock-Parker; Theresa, Matu, and Marcus Bundy; Javon Burks; Spencer Burnette; Aletheia D. and Aiesha Z. Burrell; Courtlyn and Cameron Burris; Keon Burton; Aniyah N. Butler; Coree Butler; Herman Butler; Kiera Butler; Jordan Nicole Butterfield; Athena, Michael, Ian, and Meera Buxton; Gina Marie Byrd; Robert Cage; Leila Calhoun; Darren Cambridge; Briana Campbell; Derrick Camper; Myles, Devin, and Loryn Canty; Denise Carey; Kiera Carey; Charles E. and Charlotte E. Carlies; Samuel and Megan Carmichael; Darron L. Carpenter; Jesse Carpenter, Jr.; Christopher Carr; Jalaya Carter; Jhasmyne Carter; Niyla Elajah Carter;

Timothy Cathcart; Isabella Cazenave; Ingrid Chancellor; Nzinga, Lateefah, Akilah, and Orlando Chandler; Zik and Cheo Chandler; Alexius Chapman; Tmya Chappell; Kamari Michael Charles; Preston Michael Chenault; Sydney and Chelsea Chester; Marianna Christian; Alexis Clark; Brenda A. Clark-McIntyre; Brice Clark; Michael, Logan, and Joshua Clark; Navar Tyrei Clark; Ricky Clark; Bryson Clarke; Christian Clarke; Christian Jayden Clarke; Tiffani Clarke; Ramon, Azairiyia, and Alireya Clayton; Anthony Cockrell; Leilani Jade Code; Danielle Coleman; Maalachi Coleman; Laila Collins; Richelle Collins; D. J., Takesha R., and Oliver Conday; Tonea and Christopher Conley, Zaria Ambers, Joshua and Makiah Conley, Kiera Profit, and Destiny Griffin; Casey Connerly; Tiara Nicole Cooper and Aleesa Jenell Hackley; Destiny Copeland; Allencia Kyri Cotten; Lauryn Alexandra Cottman; Ahamarianna Cov; Whigham Rachel Covington; Layla Cozart-Amos; Bria and Christian Crawford; Kayla Crawford with Jasmine and Jordan Jackson; Tahron Crawford; Dominique Creese; Louis Creese; Sa'Miah Crockett; Raven Crowe; Starr Jermaine Cunningham; Debbie Curley; LaDawn Curley; Jacelyn Curtis; Tristan Elise Cyrus; Timberly Dabney-Bryant; Joshua Daggett; Cameron Tyree Dail; Taylor Alice Renee and Carlton William Daley, III; DaAnthony Daniel; Chayce Daniels; Jaylyn Deneice Daniels; Alyssa Darden; Ciara Darden; Elijah Dariah; Landon Darjean; Malcolm and Malik Dash; Taylor Danielle Daugherty; Andrea Elizabeth Davis; Lamount Davis and Janae' Sims; Mariah Davis; Mildred Davis's granddaughters: Enfynnati, Rhianne, Sadiyya, and Lailaa; Myra D. Davis; Payton Howard Davis; Shayla Ashanti Davis; Justin Dominic Dean; Jadon Denard; Khari A. Dennis; La Neice, Cory, La Niya, Erick, Jr., William, and La Nae Dennis; Jamal Sanoussy Diakite, Jerel Devarron Jackson, Kamaria Nicole Willis, and Denisha Dear; DeShuna Dickens; Ryan Dickson; Alexis and Alex Diggs; Endeah Dillard; Harrison Milton Dillard; Marissa Elese Dillard; Jordan and Mia Dixon; Chynna Marie Dock; Samantha and Jennifer Dominguez; Dominique Dorsett; Lora N. Douglas; Tamyra Khloe Douglas; Tarmen Lee Douglas, III; Towrence Marquell Douglas; Madison Rose Drake; Madison Draper; Tariq and Xavier Drayton; Alicia Duerson; Jaden Carol Duke; Jonna Marie Dukes; Brantley Damon Dumas, II; Tara Louise Dunk; Issiah and Quiara Dunson; Ahmya and Jordan Duplessis; Kassius Dante Duplessis; Alyssa Durham, Brady and Daniel Dyson; Michaela and Zion Durham; Jacob Eakins; Dayvion and Jayvion Edmond-Gregory; Braylon Edwards; Karsten Edwards; Myles Aiden Edwards; Alivia and Nevaeh Eggleston; Alyscia N. El-Amin; Jarel L. Ellis; Meaghan Ellis; Kiyana and Michael

Ellison; Malik Ellison; Amarah Ennis; Sierra Jona Espinoza; Xavier Essex; Kennedi Kenisha Essien; Ashley Jade Eugene; Imani Cimone Evans; Juan, Desmond, and Imani Evereteze; Bryce Elijah Falker; Taylor Brienna Farrell; Indigo Ahsanti, Cyann Azure, Navi Anais, and Skye Ylana Ferdinand; Brianna Ferguson; Jaylyn Madisen Ferrell; Jazzeria', Michael, Damonaires, Scotticheal, Quantasia, Damonasha, Di, Daquaria', and Regina Ferrell; Kalicia and Robert Fields; Torry Fields; Walter D. Files, Jr.; Mason Fils; Yenga Fiteu; Jocoya and Jahmir Flowers; Kathy Floyd-Buggs; Ryann and Regann Flynn; Sacha Adaher Flynn; Khalil Foley; Nathan Forbes; Evan LaMonte Ford; Johnathon Forrest; Trinity Foster; Taylor Fournillier; Karenda, Carlos, Lynnelle, Charletta, Kanetha, and Kashon Fowler; Kilas Christopher Francis; Diamond "Zora" Nichole Francois; Zaria and Zaniya Francois; Gregory, Jackie, and Rosalyn Franklin; Jahmir Franklin; Adrienne Frazier; Christianna Frazier; Akilah Freeman; Lauren and RJ Freeman; Marley Ndey Freeman; Alexaundria Fretty; Sydney Ariel Fretty; DeAndre Fulgham; Nicholas Fulgham; Janell, Terry, and Saniyah Gaddis; Dailyn Gaines; Kamaria Gardner; Alexis Makayla Garmon; Briana Garmon; Annalese Garner; Cassandra Garner; Sydney Simone Garrett; Jaxon Shandon Gay; Irving Gelzer; Jonathan Christian George; Gilbert K. Ghand; Dashaun Gibson; Aanazisha Gilbert; "Baby Daughter" Gilmore (at a prenatal 16 weeks!); JaKobie Lamar Ginns; Jaylan Glenn; Aniyah Da'Naysa Glover; Jeremy Goodie and Darienne McKenzie; Andrew Gordon, Audrey Thames, and Arika Thames; Dillon Michael Gousby; Jada C. Graham; Katelyn Graham; VonCile Graham; Harley Grands; Chandler Nicole and James Alford Grant, III; Monica Graves; Anthony V. Green, Jr.; Kiersten Green; Theautry Green; Sierra and Grayson Gregg; Timothy James Griffin; Rhiley Grooms; Dwayne and Cierra Gross; Jabari Gross; Kamaria Gross; Kyla Grove; Jaden and Moses Guidry; Janice and Barbara Guient; RogLynn and LaChia Gunter; Maya Naomi Das Gupta

H–O

Raina Hairston; Aaron and Andre' Hall; Christopher Jerome Hall, II; Dorian Michael Hall; Kimoni Kwei Hall; Minnie Hamm's grandchildren: Kha-Lyse and Ya-Zaria Hamm-Smith, Briana Devon Hamm, and Karon Smith; Quinn Hammond; Jasmine Delores Hammonds; Jada Haney; Devin Trey Jimmie Hankins; Justin Marvin Hankins; Jared and Jaiden Hardeman; Maddox and Manning Harper; Jordan Harrington; Carol and Cassie Harris; Damien Harris; Esaiah Harris; Jada, Makayla, and

Kierstyn Harris; Khari Teshome Harris; Simone A. Harris; Timia Harris; Jayden Michael Hartley; Madison Rai Hatley; Chanelle Hatton and Jade Erin DeLilly; VaShawn Hayes; Sinaiya Hazell; "Baby" Haywood (not quite ready to leave the womb!); Harrison Head; Nira Elizabeth Headen; Bryce Kaylen Heard; Alexys, Kyleese, and Xenia Henderson; Capri and Courtney Henderson-Glover; Kaleb and Jaden Henderson; Stephen Henson; Jahlil and Camryn Herring; Aaron, Austin, and Corey Hicks; Brandon M. Hicks; Tiara Hicks; Aundraya Hill; Christian Hill; Hayden Addison Hill; Rashida Maciana and Macio Hoggins Hill, III; Sapphire Hill; Skyler Nia Hill; Charlton Jairus Hilliard; Cymone Shemari and Taylor Hoffman; Josiah Wesley Hogan; Jamal Mandela Holley; Joshua, Jessica, and Justin Holley and Alexis Diaz; Tyler James Holloman; Julia Holmes; Joseph Ellis Hood; Judah Hooper; Cheyenne House, Mikayla Sykes, Treasure Dearing, and Dyshallies Holmes; Darius Howard; Mac III, Makenzie, and Bria Howard; Aaron Howell; Dinari Frank Hudson; Jayden Hulett; Christopher and Justice Hunt; Kiana, Kaitlyn, and Kyla Hunter; Robyn Denise Hurst; Chandler Ross Hutcherson; Frederick James Isaac, III; Quinesia Isabel; James Alexander and Camiyon Betyne Isaiah; Briana, Gregory, Khalil, and Margeaux Ivy; Aaron Jack; Andre C. Jackson; Caleb and Victoria Jackson; Chelsea Nandi and Dwayne Akil Jackson; Clinton O'Neal Jackson, III; Delbert C. Jackson; Elijah Reese Jackson; Isaiah James Jackson; Isaiah Keir Jackson; Jamond Jackson; Jeremiah Keir Jackson; Laiya Jackson; Leonard Jackson, III; Marcus Jackson; Maria Jackson; Sydney Jackson; Taea and Talia Jackson; Tamiko C. Jackson; Tyler Jamal Jackson; Wyndell, Tehron, and Kimani Jackson; Will and Malik Jacobs; Christopher and Chrishenia James; Juwan Sandtez Jamison and Jacob Derrick Jamison Kiwanuka; Solomon Aderes Jammer; Khafil Hakeem Jefferson; London James Jemison; Symien Myles Jemison; Jessica and Derrick Jenkins, Jr.; Kaleb Jessie; Alanna and Amachi Johnson; Alese and Trileise Johnson; Braydan Chanah Johnson; Bryce Channing and Bray Toya Johnson; Damian Johnson; Hassan Johnson; Jeremaine Johnson; Jeremy and Veronica Johnson; KaSean Johnson; Layton Johnson, Jr.; Nia Johnson; Paige Johnson; Patrice and Pamela Johnson; Taylor Johnson; Tristan Johnson; Ursel and Ursula Johnson; Veronica Johnson; Xavier Tiberius Johnson; Zuri Johnson; Aneisa Jones; Angel E. Jones; Charli Jones; Christopher W., III, Crysta Renee, and Corey Jones; Cidney, Ron, Justice, Janice, and Milton Jones; Ethan Jones; JaLesa, Derrick, and JaKaylah Jones; Janae and Nya Jones; Jeremiah Patrick Jones; Jevonna, Aleena, and Caleb Jones; Lyric and Lacey Jones; Madison Jae Jones; Marcus Jones, Jr.; Miles Jones-Patton;

Patricia and Ronnie Jones; Rae and Daisy Jones; Roger Jones; Vanessa and Chucky Jones; Kaylin Alexandria and Cameron Alexander Jordan; Sidney Jordan; Ethan Xavier Joyce; Hannah Gabrielle Judon; Anson, Adams, and Aaron Karmo; Bobby Michel Kelly; J'Naya B. Kelly; Kaden Banks Kelly; Kaden Parker Kelly; Jared Kemp; Alisha R. Kennedy; Jackie Kennedy, Ande Bushell, Marcus Gibson, and Jamal Freeman; Tobias Anton Kennedy; Zoey Amirah Kenney; Brian W. Kerr, Jr.; Jada Kidd-Asoera; Jaden Phillip King; Kameron and Kavanna King; Khayla Charnise King; Lauren and Blair King; Allison Kinnard; Sean Donovan Kirce; Demetrius Kirkland; Amaya Janae Kirkpatrick; Leah Pearce Koonce; Zamira L. Kornegay; Zarin Alonzo Kornegay; Malcolm and Malik Lacey; Asali Lacy; Diamond Lacy and Khaiya Lewis; Djimon Kea' Lam; Amina Lamar; Antwain Lambert; Derrick Lambert; Tasha Lambert; Quinn Patricia Langford, Renelle Theresa and Burnell Goins Langie; Sydney Maria Lanier; Noelle Lanton; Quentin Lark; Qadre Latiker; Ricky Lauture; Muriel Leach; Jahzzir Lee; Shenika Lee; Tytiauna Leslie; Summer Leverette; Alisha Lewis and Teri Ward; Benet and BreAnna Lewis; Kaleb E. Lewis; Krystal Lewis; Mekhi Keith Lewis; Ty Isaiah Lewis; Brooke K. Liddell; Jason Liddell; Genesis Elease Lightfoot; Kamilah Lindsey; Shakira Lindsey; Gavin Littlejohn; Saran Lloyd; Mazie Tertulia Loayza; Jazzlynn Locklear and Bryson Carr; Jordan Lofton; DaiJah and Kallayah Logan; Mia and Maya Long; Angel, Tia, and Kimani Longmire; Chris, III, Crysta, and Corey Lowery; Darrell, Jordan, and Jalen Lucas; Ernest, Royce, and Rensea Lunsford; Alejandro McAllister; Kenneth, Linda, Kenley-Shemeka, Armand, and Ramond McBeth; Charlise Lyn McCall; Damion and Jasmyne McCauther; Christopher J. McClellan; Anne McCormick and Kaia Brock; Corbin Michael McCoy; Elijah Jahiem McCutcheon; Morgan McDaniel; Bradley McDonald; Willie Nelson McEntee; Freeman Christian McGahee; Amanda McKendrick; Jayden Alexis McKinney; Rae Ann McLean; Evan Asbury McMillan; Denise McNair; Trinity McNear; Kairie Simone MaGee; Joshua Major; Nicholas Malbreaux; Mateen M. Mamou; Rodney Noah Mangham; Hayley Kyliece Manning; Joshua Manning, Tyenne Fulton-Crosson, Aaron Manning, Adrielle Fulton-Crosson, and Jordan Fulton; Victoria Alexis Manning; Gabriel Akil Rollins Marrero; Naia Ellison Reese Marrow; Amira Wesley Marshall; Kristian Myrtlee and Anthony Dewayne Marshall, Jr.; Bryana Martin; Christopher Evan Martin; Jason T. Martin; Kimberly Martin; Marlon Martin; Victoria Linette Martin; Rania Alicia Martinez; Tracy Martika Martinez, Jr.; Antonio Mason, Jr.; Vallen Mata; Aubri Mathews; Jac'Quise, Miyah, and Aaliya Matlock; Iyanna Matthews; Jaelin La'Mar and Erin Jordanette Matthews; Dalen Craig May; Taisha Mayberry; Gabrielle and Trinity Mayes; Britnee K. Maynor; Larrun J. Maynor; Christian Mays, Raeden N. Mays; TaTyana Mays; Kahnleigh Meaux; Imani Gabriel MeNeese; Jennifer Merriweather; Brooke and Benjamin Meshack, II; Khristopher Issac Mewa; Mathieu Steuart Mewa; Mikayla Rhys Mewa; Joshua Alexander Mickles; Taylor Ann Elizabeth Mike; Jacob William Patrick Miles; Aaron and Mackenzie Miller; Brandon Miller; Christopher J. Miller, Jr.; Donalee Miller; Gyasi Miller; Trinity and Israel Miller; Perry Milsap; Peyton R. Milsap; Damien Minniefield; ZaLeigh, Faith, and Jedan Minnifield; Cheryl Minyard's grandchildren: Melissa A. Minyard, Michael A. Shelton, Jaleel Patterson, Brittany Minyard, Mercedes Minyard, James Minyard, II, Janai Minyard, Michon Minyard, and Mark Patterson; Aniya Mitchell; Jaleesa Mitchell; John Henry Mitchell, III; Julian, Jared, and Johnathan Mitchell; Olexia DeEvelyn Mitchell; Eula Malyimo Mlay; Erin Nicole Moody; Dalen Moore; Karrington Shantrece Moore; Nickolas Moore; Soriah Jordan Moore; MaliVai James and Amiri Imari Morgan; Will Morgan, III; Thomas E. Morris; Ranisha, Shonte', Deonte', and Desir Moss; Simone and Darius Moss, Jr.; Zuheera Muhammad and Darren and Darlanda Muhammad; Skyler Mukes; Ta'Nya Muldrew; Nia and Nathan Munford; Marcus Murphy, Jr.; Kali Rosetta Murry; Zaiya Kai Murry; Thurston Delane Muskelly, II; Cora Elyse Myers; Jayden Parker Myers; Sion Myles; Darryl Jacob Narcisse; Michael Anthony Narcisse; Alvin, Jr., Letitia, Alicia, and Ebony Nelson; Isaiah Hall Newsom; Cole Nathaniel Nichols; Breland Norwood; Kristen Marie Norwood; Jalen North; Allen Nunes; Aysha Nunes; Sam O'Bryant; Carlyse Landa Olds; Amara-Nicole, Aiyana Nichelle, and Aryssa Gabrielle Oliver; Alaysia, Mireyna, and Noah Pauline Orejel; Kavon Owens; Xavier Owens; Zoje Owinge; Olorunnifise O. Owoade; Akinsola, Ifaseeyen, and Abiola Oyewale

P–Z

Elry F. Pacheco, Jr.; Valentino and Kieshia Paige; Chelsea Paige Palmer; Jada Palmer; Khadijah Ali Palmer; James Davis Paramore, III; Jaela Hope Parham; Isaiah Sirron Paris; Skyler and Carter Parker; Kenzi Micah Curette Patton; Robert Paul, Jr.; Amaiya Payne; Bennie Leon Payne, III; Amya Pearson; Cheka B. Pedescieaux; Tara Rene Pellerin; Jalen I. Perkins; Joseph G. Perkins, V; La'Kya Mornae Perkins; William Jackson Perkins; Artwau Perry, Jr.; Amirah Nalani Peters; Kenneth Peters; Camille Joycelyn Pettway; Jalen Philips; Angela Pierce; Michael

Pierce; Tranesa and Errol Pierre, with Kaden Harnett; Daron Pines; Joseph Christian Piquant; Megan Pitt; Kierston and Kendal Pitts; Chelsie Elizabeth Ann Poindexter; Christopher Ethan Poindexter; Jamani Tyree' Pollard; Jeremy Pollard-Johnson; Marissa Renea Poole; Chandler Pope; Demi M. Porter; Wesley and Tiera Powe with Tasheena and Delvera Hinds; Gionni Premeci; Morgan Price; Gwendolyn Pride; Jirah L. Pruitt; Robert N. Prymus, III; Eian Duane Gregory Pugh; Evan Michael Pugh; Randi A. Quarles; Carryn D. Queeley-Gibson; Khalil Ramone; Raymond, II, and Ryland Randle; Howard DaShon Randolph; Arriq M. Redd; Coutney Redfern; Jasia N. Redmond; Carlos Reed; Donovan and Chanelle Reese; Madison Reid; Jahlil Rice; Lauren Richards; Jazine and MauriAnna Richardson, Darnell and Rianon Wallace, and David Fant; Jessie Richardson, Jr.; Nancy Jean Kaye Richardson; Maknazeh R. Richee; Lauryn Ashley Rivers; Mikayla Roache; Kamari Rene Robertson; April Robinson; Charles Robinson, Sr.; Dante R. Robinson; Fabian, Karen, and Martin Robinson; Jeanette Robinson; Morgan Robinson; Ridwaan and Yayah Robinson; Sydney TaMya Roby; Sammie L. Rogers, Jr., Tremaine J. Love, and Tevin L. Love; Asha Roland; Trinity Rose, Talandra Jones, and Shanteria Rose; Jaylon Emerson Roseboro; Cameron Adonius Rosette-Driver; Morgan Ross; Trenton Everett Ross; Theresa, Joe, and Tonya Rousey; Davis Anthony Rowe; Lindsay Dallas Royston; Gregory A. Ruffin; Mathew Horace Runderson; Horace L. Russell, III; Bakary Saho; Alexandria McKenzie and Michael Jeffrey Sanders; Kenneth Charles Sanders, III; Koryn Sanders; Yahney-Marie Sangare; Cameron Sapp; Nia Rochelle Sapp; Nina Simone Sapp (in womb/34 weeks); Elijah, Sydni, and Madison Saunders; Tamar Arielle Saunders; Alex Thomas and Aleia Victoria Scott; Ashanti Lonel Scott; Jamaal Allen Scott; Janel Ayana Scott; Ladonna Scott; Sonya Scott; Allecia Segar; Shaun Selmore; Danielle Session; Joyce Sharpe; Kai, Kwameh, and Ayanni Sharpe; Monique Sharpe; Jasmine and Brianna Shavon; Cara and Blair Sherman; Christiana Shumpert; Kobe and Zaria Sifflet; Deinaria Ayanna Silas; Cameron Simeon-Major; Maliyah Simmons; Kennedie Vashti Sims; Janiya B. and James Singleton, III; Willis Joseph Singleton, Jr.; Samuel and Sienna Slaughter; Gabrielle Smalls; Alessandra Smith, Alexander Smith, Brandon Brown, and Ava Lewis; Amber Smith; Asia Z. Smith, Kiara S. Hinton-Griffin, Winston J. Griffin, and Keam J. Leonard; Ashton and Joi Smith; Ayanna Smith, Carlos Smith, Taelore Hicks, and Nailah Hicks; Brendan, Porsche, and James Smith; Darreahn and Devinn Smith; Deandre Smith, Chancy Allen, Brittney, Zion Harris, and Zoi Harris; Doanna Smith; Donald Smith, Jr.; Hunter and Jazper

Smith; Jasmine and Johnny Smith; Jean Smith; Jewel and Christian Smith; Juwan Gregory Smith; Khayla Smith; Leonard Morris and Paul Smith; Leslie Smith; London Smith; Messiah and Sidney Smith; Morris Lekeith Smith II; Stephanie Smith; TreShay Smith; Yanessa Michelle Smith; Michael and Makayla Sneed; Blake Sterling Solomon, II; Brandi and Brittani Solomon; Ciarra and Anthony Solomon; Tayler Anisa Jene Southall; Micaela and Amy Sparks; Achebe Spencer; Bea Springfield; Ahmad St. John, Ariana Poindexter, Kamari Gallaman, Jordan Pipkin, and Jaquan Poindexter; Arrin and Amber Stallings; Daniel and Noelle Steele; S. Caleb Steele; Liam Gregory Stegall; Adrianna Stephens; Caleb and Zuri Stephens; Lela Stevens; Marty and Sydnee Stevens; Kendrick Isaiah Stevenson; Damia Faith Steward; Dyani Steward; Desmond X. Stewart; Gabrielle Marie Naloni' Stewart; Ajani Stowers; Aric Tyler Styles; Lauryn Sudduth; Dueri Perry Sullivan; Corey B. Summers; Taylor Summers; Zenzi Summers; Domonique Sumner; Akeili Bella Danil Sutton; Ja'Nyra Simone Sutton; Mylesha Swindell; Quentin and Lauren Sykes; Rebecca Tailor; Ja'atea Tate; Kamaria Yuri Taylor; Xavier Taylor and Christopher Jackson; Zania Taylor; MacKenzie Simone Telfaire; Dominic Tennial and Devin Slocum; Jaden Terah; Angel Terry; Kambre Terry; Kamden Terry; Deshara Thomas; Jayla Simone Thomas; J. Calvin Thomas; Kiara Thomas; Niko and Narayan Thomas; Raven Simone Thomas; SaNanda Thomas; Tyran Lamar Thomas; Evan Troyan and Ethan James Thompson; Jasper and Carlie Thompson; R. J. Thompson; Sasha Thornton; Tanya Tibby; Adrian Munengi Timmons; Ashley Charmaine Tisdale; Wykhia Janae Toombs; David and Helaine Torregano; Camille Trent; Anaya and Amir Troy; Joshua and Justin Tuck; Barak Joseph Gerard Tucker; Bryce Rashad Turner; Derrick, Derron, and Christina Turner, with Johnathan and Courtney Clark and Renesea Guess; Ashley Tyler; Evan and Aaron Tyler; Ashley, Leni, and Leonard Tyson; Indra Valdez; Angel Vasquez and Elias Stewart; Adelphe Vaughn-Carpenter; Gabriel Vega; Aiyah Vickers; Azarye Mateo Wade; Torry Wade and Devion D. Williams; Dan and Taye Walden; Angelica Beryl Walker; Audi Walker; Kennedye Renee Walker; Kimani Walker; Sarah Walker; Kaci Wall; Rodney, Kayla, and Latoya Wall; Destiny Waller; Sara Ward, Brenda McIntyre, Courtney Douglas, and Lora Douglas; Seth Ward; Crystal, Kennedy, and Ryan Ware; Reginald B. Ware; Derrick, Jarrin, and Channing Warren; Allen McCovey Washington; Ebony Washington; Joshua Washington; JoyKendra Washington and Jadyn Lee; Samiah "Brittany" Monique Washington; Solomon Washington; Jasmyne Waters; Gabrielle Watkins; Ian Benjamin Watkins; Brian Watson; Ezion Watson; Olivia

Awele Watson; R. Camron Waugh; Angela Weathers; E. L., Marshall, LaDena, Angeline, Augusta, and Jessye Weathers; Lavada Weathers; Aisha, Patricia, and Kevin Weathersby; Devin-Danielle Webb; Alan David Webster, III; Jayden Welch; Anthony Isaiah Wells; D'Aylin Celestine Wells; Andrew Wesley; Sydney West; Taylor Skye West; Aaron Westbrook; Stephanie Westbrook; Tajir, Amos, Denver, Zion, and Jadyn Wharton; Ashlynn Diane White; Donyae Janel and Khouri Brenae White; Jalil White; Jase White; Jikeela and Tyuana White, Raven Sampson, and Tashariah Sampson; Kadence A. and Carson A. White; Ramazzi White; Sydney TaMya White; Timothy Benjamin and Samuel Goodman White; Tyrone and Tyrell White; Zharia Rose Marie and Zachary Rodrequez White, Jr.; Kennedi C.P. Whitener-Mason; Zachary Scott Wiedeback; Malaya Serenity Wiggins; Eric Wilcox II; Marlon P. Wilkins; Tashon T. Wilkins; Aalayah Williams; Addison Joplin Williams; Alexandriana Noelani Eldora Williams; Alix Williams; Atiya, Jaleel, Jahari, and Eldred Williams, Jr.; Brandon Williams; Bree Williams; Candace, Jasmine, Chelsea, Kayla, and Jordan Williams; Chicara Faith Williams; Devinti M. Williams, II; Dezden Williams; Georrail Williams; Gregory Williams; Illeyse Williams; Jordan Williams; Jordan Daniel Williams; Keith Alexander and Xavier Quinton Williams; Leo Williams; LuVora Arnette Williams; Morghan Rachel Williams; T. J. Williams; Kayla Willis; Anatesha Wilson; Dominic Wilson; Zoi, Zion, Zaria, Chancy, Britney, and DeAndre Wilson; Elijah Damiel, Asa Nehemiah, and Colin Alexander Winborne; Taylor Winn; Jasmine Michelle Winnegan; Durriyah Wisham; Cameron Woodard; Courtney Woodard; Kaley Requel Wooding-Lewis; Caliyah, Victoria, and Trinity Woods; Devon Dior Worth; Jaiya Renae Worthy; Kathleen M. Wright; Matara LuTrise Wright; William Grant Wright; Elijah Yates; Ian Stanton Young; Jayvon D'Lawrence Young; Julian Markail Young; Waverly Yves; Allston and Avery Zanders

THE COVENANT *In Action* was produced in collaboration with PolicyLink and The Jamestown Project.

PolicyLink Headquarters
1438 Webster
Suite 303
Oakland, CA 94612
www.policylink.org

The Jamestown Project
1140 Chapel Street
Suite 301
New Haven, CT 06510
www.JamestownProject.org

ABOUT TAVIS SMILEY

With his late-night television talk show, *Tavis Smiley,* on PBS, and his radio show *The Tavis Smiley Show* from NPR, **Tavis Smiley** was the first American ever to simultaneously host signature talk shows on both PBS and National Public Radio. Smiley's television program is the first show in the history of PBS to be broadcast from the West Coast. *The Tavis Smiley Show* on public radio is currently distributed by PRI, Public Radio International, and his weekly podcast is offered at **www.TavisTalks.com.** Additionally, Tavis offers political commentary on the nationally syndicated *Tom Joyner Morning Show.*

Tavis has authored numerous books, including *On Air* and *What I Know For Sure: My Story of Growing Up in America,* a searing memoir of poverty, ambition, and, ultimately, atonement. He's also the founder of the Tavis Smiley Foundation.

Website: **www.TavisTalks.com.**

ABOUT CORNEL WEST

Dr. **Cornel West** is the Class of 1943 University Professor of Religion at Princeton University. Prior to his Princeton appointment, he taught at Yale, Union Theological Seminary, and was the Alphonse Fletcher Jr. University Professor at Harvard University, where he taught Afro-American Studies and the Philosophy of Religion. He is the author of numerous articles and 20 books including the best-selling *Democracy Matters* and *Race Matters*. His latest project is Street Revelations, a spoken-word compilation CD (Hidden Beach). As one of America's most gifted and provocative public intellectuals, West is a widely sought-after speaker and guest lecturer at colleges and universities across the country.

We hope you enjoyed this Smiley Books/Hay House publication.
If you would like to receive additional information, please contact:

SMILEY
BOOKS

Hay House, Inc.
P.O. Box 5100
Carlsbad, CA 92018-5100

(760) 431-7695 or **(800) 654-5126**
(760) 431-6948 (fax) or **(800) 650-5115 (fax)**
www.hayhouse.com® • **www.hayfoundation.org**

Tune in to **HayHouseRadio.com®** for the best in inspirational
talk radio featuring top Hay House authors! And, sign up via
the Hay House USA Website to receive the Hay House online
newsletter and stay informed about what's going on
with your favorite authors. You'll receive bimonthly
announcements about: Discounts and Offers,
Special Events, Product Highlights, Free
Excerpts, Giveaways, and more!
www.hayhouse.com®